'Justin Brierley stands at the top of those who host high-quality podcasts on religious matters. His years of experience dialoguing with believers and non-believers alike on countless topics, and doing so intelligently and with congeniality, makes him the perfect person to write this book. This book is a great read, engaging as well as educational, and will encourage one to think deeply about the issues covered. Moreover, by the time readers reach the end of the book, they will feel as though they have become friends with its author. Highly recommended!'

Michael Licona, Associate Professor of Theology
Houston Baptist University, Texas

'This is a highly readable survey of the reasons for Christian faith, often called "apologetics". But it is not just an academic exercise. Justin has respectfully engaged many thoughtful atheists and sceptics over the years, which is always a test for a believer. The book is therefore very personal – it explains how his own faith has emerged while working through the challenges he has received. Believers and non-believers (and the many in between) will all be helped by this volume.'

Tim Keller, Redeemer Presbyterian Church, New York City

'A wonderfully clear, winsome and accessible case for Christianity from a man who has hosted many of the world's most prominent sceptics and atheists. The mixture of storytelling and argument is engaging, and the result is compelling.'

Andrew Wilson, church leader, author, theologian
and co-host of the Mere Fidelity *podcast*

'Atheists tell us that they are champions of reason. If so, how does a man who each week hears the arguments of the world's most articulate atheists remain a committed Christian? Unbelievable? No, Justin Brierley is just marvellously well informed (and well mannered). Here he takes us behind the scenes of his popular radio debates between atheists and Christians to show us why his Christian beliefs are stronger than ever. A beautifully written cure for doubts and a spirited defence of Christianity.'

Frank Turek, author, speaker and radio host of Cross Examined

'Above all else, this book shows the moral decency of Justin Brierley. He quotes me saying that, although a non-believer, my life has been guided by the Parable of the Talents. He could have quoted me saying that, in the *Republic*, Plato says that the full life is one of sharing. Read this delightful book and see how Justin Brierley walks in the paths of both Athens and Jerusalem.'

Michael Ruse, Lucyle T. Werkmeister Professor of Philosophy and Director of the Program in the History and Philosophy of Science Department of Philosophy, Florida State University

'Beautifully written, brilliantly argued, Justin's book *Unbelievable?* will thrill Christians and challenge atheists. Everyone should read this book and buy extra copies to give away.'

R. T. Kendall, author and pastor

'Over the past decade, I've come to recognize *Unbelievable?* with Justin Brierley as a show of unparalleled quality. Week by week, Brierley facilitates in-depth conversational debate across deep ideological divides with just the right balance between rigour and accessibility. The same may be said of Justin's new book. Fans of *Unbelievable?* will find here a treasure trove of insights and reflections mined from a decade of hosting debates on life's biggest questions. But Justin's book is not simply a backstage pass to his fine radio show; it stands on its own as an eloquent, accessible and winsome apologetic in the grand tradition of C. S. Lewis.'

Randal Rauser, theologian, author and blogger, Alberta, Canada

'Whether you are a believer or a seeker, this book is a must-read. Through the lens of his popular radio show *Unbelievable?*, Brierley invites readers to consider the evidence for the Christian faith. He not only lays out a powerful case for Christianity, but does so in an interesting, judicious and entertaining fashion. Here's my suggestion: get a copy, read it and then discuss it with a friend.'

Sean McDowell, Assistant Professor of Apologetics,
Biola University, California, and a popular speaker and author
of over 15 books, including A New Kind of Apologist

'Gracious, thoughtful conversations about matters of belief and unbelief are very valuable – but, sadly, all too rare in today's culture of memes, sarcasm, and hostile attack and counter-attack. Can we do better? Justin Brierley says yes – and has ten years of fruitful conversations as the host of *Unbelievable?* to prove it. Here, he offers a twofold apologetic: first, he gives reasons why he is indeed still a Christian after all those conversations with atheists; second, he demonstrates that genuine dialogue is both possible and fruitful. Written in an engaging, relaxed style, his book will be useful and encouraging for Christians who are trying to find ways to talk about their faith with sceptical friends and family, and it will be an interesting and thought-provoking read for sceptics as well.'

Dr Holly Ordway, author of
Not God's Type: An Atheist Academic Lays Down Her Arms

'After ten years of interviewing atheists and agnostics, Justin Brierley has heard every argument there is against God and the Christian faith, yet he is unpersuaded; what's more, he is more confident in his faith than ever before! In *Unbelievable?* Justin guides the reader by the hand with his well-researched and carefully argued thesis, persuasively showing that Christianity makes the best sense of the world around us. In a world ruptured by cultural fragmentation and competing ideologies, Justin is credible because he has shown us how to cultivate important and necessary conversations in a winsome way with people we disagree with, without being disagreeable; reflecting the spirit of Jesus, who himself asked over one hundred questions in the Gospels. Indeed, evidence mixed with authentic Christian experience is the core of a vibrant faith that has allowed Justin to address a very important topic and bless the Church with this uniquely important book.'

Jeremiah J. Johnston, President of the Christian Thinkers Society and Professor of Early Christianity, Houston Baptist University, Texas

'This provocative title draws the reader into Justin Brierley's story. By describing debates and dialogues between well-known critics, such as Richard Dawkins, Bart Ehrman and Richard Carrier, and well-known Christian apologists, Brierley reflects on accounts from perhaps the best-known religious dialogue programme today. Hundreds of archives retell these major skirmishes. As one of his guests and the subject of a chapter in this volume, I can attest first-hand to Justin's well-placed questions, engaging follow-up and even-handed treatment. So why is Justin still a Christian? Join this highly recommended conversation and enjoy the answers that he provides!'

Gary R. Habermas, Distinguished Research Professor and Chair, Philosophy Department, Liberty University, Virginia

'Against the rising tide of the "New Atheism" since the millennium, there has arisen a new wave of thinking Christians, unabashed and unashamed to defend the faith and assert their confidence in a living Christ. Justin is one of those. He has hosted his radio show *Unbelievable?* for the past ten years, and has had ample opportunity to listen to lively conversations and debate between atheists and Christians (many of them household names among academics). These conversations have resulted in Justin re-examining his Christian beliefs and discovering that he is more committed to their veracity than ever. He has become very skilled himself at answering objections to the faith, but maintains warmth and respect towards those who disagree with him.

This is a friendly, clear, relational book discussing the central tenets of the Christian faith. It is eminently readable. I loved it, and I hope you will too.'

Faith Forster, co-founder of Ichthus Christian Fellowship

'Ten years of dialoguing with sceptics has given Justin Brierley a unique insight into the questions and issues that divide atheists and Christians. In *Unbelievable?*, Justin helps Christians to understand their atheist friends, treat their questions seriously, and comprehend how to give answers with depth, clarity and compassion. A deeply thoughtful, incredibly generous book that encourages Christians to take seriously the task of not only answering our sceptical friends but also of truly listening to them.'

Andy Bannister, Director, Solas Centre for Public Christianity
and author of The Atheist Who Didn't Exist

'Finally! One of my favourite thinkers is now one of my favourite authors! Weaving together science, philosophy and human experience, Justin offers reasons for God's existence that are both personal and deeply thoughtful. The result is beautifully compelling. There is honesty and gentleness in these pages, pulled from thousands of on-air conversations with guests of all kinds of belief and lack thereof. Justin's first-hand, front-line experience has really paid off: *Unbelievable?* is an incredible work that deserves the widest possible readership.'

Bruxy Cavey, Teaching Pastor, The Meeting House and author of The End of Religion *and* Reunion: The Good News of Jesus for Seekers, Saints, and Sinners

'Writing with the same clarity he brings to radio discussions, Justin has a way of cutting to the nub of issues that make difficult concepts understandable – even for agnostics like me!'

Mike Rand, Unbelievable? *listener*

'Civil, productive debates about religion aren't possible any more – not between Christians and atheists anyway, and *certainly* not when you put a microphone in the room. That's the conventional wisdom – and Justin Brierley has been proving it wrong every week for more than ten years. But as I've listened to the talented and gracious host of the *Unbelievable?* podcast, I've often wondered how he straddles these worlds without having his faith torn apart. *Unbelievable?* [the book] is the answer to that question, and it is rich and compelling. It will leave believers and sceptics more open to conversations with each other, and seekers more impressed with the truth and beauty of the Christian faith.'

Drew Dyck, acquisitions editor at Moody Publishers, Senior Editor at CTPastors.com and author of Generation Ex-Christian

UNBELIEVABLE?

Why, after ten years of talking with atheists, I'm still a Christian

Justin Brierley

First published in Great Britain in 2017

Society for Promoting Christian Knowledge
36 Causton Street
London SW1P 4ST
www.spck.org.uk

British Library Cataloguing-in-Publication Data
A catalogue record for this book is available from the British Library

ISBN 978–0–281–07798–4
eBook ISBN 978–0–281–07799–1

Typeset by Manila Typesetting Company
First printed in Great Britain by Jellyfish Solutions
Subsequently digitally printed in Great Britain

eBook by Manila Typesetting Company

Produced on paper from sustainable forests

For Lucy, Noah, Grace, Jeremy and Toby
because all my favourite conversations happen with you

Contents

Foreword

Christianity needs to reconnect with our culture, showing that faith makes sense and is able to engage the deepest questions of human existence. That's what apologetics tries to do. It sets out to engage the problems that many people clearly have with Christianity, set out the Christian faith in a faithful yet winsome way and translate our language of faith into our cultural vernacular. In this important and timely book, Justin Brierley explains how he developed his own approach to apologetics, and why this has generated such interest in both Christian and atheist circles.

In my view, the reason why Justin's Premier Christian Radio show *Unbelievable?* has had such an impact is that he is willing to engage leading atheists and take their concerns seriously. Some might see this as risky, exposing Christian audiences to alternative viewpoints which they might find threatening. Yet Christians need to realize both that their ideas need defending and that they can be defended! *Unbelievable?* sets an example to the churches, helping Christians to understand why those outside the Church sometimes find their ideas difficult, while at the same time providing an engaging, informed and persuasive Christian response.

In this book, Justin reflects on his experience in his conversations with both atheists and believers, offering a rich fare to his readers. He covers a wide range of apologetic questions, always ensuring that the atheist or secularist perspective is fairly represented, while making sure his readers know that there are good answers that can be given. This book will be a valuable resource for both those who want to think about their faith and those who want to develop these kinds of conversations themselves. As Justin makes clear, there are lots of problems with an atheist worldview. And unless we have serious yet respectful conversations with atheists, those problems will not be acknowledged. As a former atheist myself, I know how important it is for wavering atheists to find sensible and informed Christians who they can talk to about their growing doubts. I hope many wanting to have these kinds of conversations will find this book helpful and encouraging.

Alister McGrath,
Andreos Idreos Professor of Science and Religion,
University of Oxford

Acknowledgements

The poet Audre Lorde said, 'There are no new ideas. There are only new ways of making them felt.' That very much applies to this book. I don't claim to have had any new ideas about the case for God and Christianity. There are innumerable theologians, philosophers, apologists and sceptics who have had a hand in this book as I've listened, read and talked with them about faith over the years. My hope is to shape their ideas in a way that is accessible to ordinary people through telling the story of both *Unbelievable?* and my own faith journey. In the process, I hope to have created some new ways of making those ideas felt.

While there are too many names to mention that have had a background influence on this book, I must acknowledge those whose insights were a great help in the writing process. These include: Randal Rauser, whose fair-minded critiques have been so helpful; Sam Hailes, whose editorial skills are matched only by his prodigious output; members of the UK Apologetics group, especially Josh Parikh; Mike Licona for advice on Chapters 5 and 6; John Buckeridge at Premier for his advice on the writing and for his helpful steering of this project; Elizabeth Neep at SPCK for her gracious guidance through the process of writing my first book, and the many others who have been so encouraging along the way too.

Much of this book was written in Pinnock's coffee shop, in Ripley, Surrey (hands down, the best coffee shop in the world). Thanks to them for all the coffee and cake, and letting me camp out in that upstairs corner chair for so long. I also owe a debt of thanks to the *Unbelievable?* listening audience, many of whom have been with me on this journey for many years. By God's grace, I hope to travel many more years with you too.

Most importantly, I couldn't have written this book without the patience, love and support of my wife Lucy and our four children. Thank you; you mean the world to me.

Introduction

Conversations matter.

Sitting in my favourite coffee shop turns out to be an appropriate place to begin writing this book. The conversations that float across the comfy sofas and coffee tables are as diverse as the customers. Students, school mums, musicians and business professionals are all within earshot. Without trying to eavesdrop, I am soon privy to several conversations which all drift on to spirituality at some point.

Two retired male friends are talking about the current form of Chelsea FC, and whether there really is such a thing as a 'spirit world'. There are the two female students, one of whom is telling the other why she's frustrated with hearing impressive sermons at her church which don't seem to change the way people live. There is the faded hippy with long hair and a straggly beard. He's impressing the young lady opposite him with tales of environmental protests and music legends he's friends with. When their conversation turns to the power of prayer, he declares: 'It doesn't matter which religion you are; when lots of people pray it releases an energy which is bound to have an effect.'

Having conversations is one of the most important things we do in life.

I like listening to conversations and, as the host of a radio discussion show about faith, I'm lucky enough to make a living from listening to them every week. The best sort of conversations spark creativity, deepen relationships and help us to see things from another person's point of view.

Despite the frequent surveys telling us that UK churchgoing is in terminal decline and Christianity is withering away, the conversations I overheard in the coffee shop show that people are still open to talking about spiritual matters. To borrow a line from Mark Twain: 'Rumours of God's death have been greatly exaggerated.' Nevertheless, the increasing secularization of the UK and Western society in general has seen a tendency for good conversations about faith, belief and spirituality to be increasingly squeezed out of the public sphere.

From the start of the new millennium, a wave of popular books proclaiming that faith is a delusion and religion is bad for people, and how science has replaced superstitious thinking, led to the coining of the phrase the 'New Atheism'. That movement, unofficially headed by the biologist Richard Dawkins, the journalist the late Christopher Hitchens, and public intellectuals from the USA such as Sam Harris and Daniel Dennett, has been widely chronicled and their influence continues to be widespread.

Much of my professional career has been spent debating the ideas and objections levelled at Christian faith by these men and their sizeable audience. However, the tone of their books has been so dismissive of religion it's no surprise that many people who read them end up being persuaded that sensible conversations with people of faith are a non-starter. As Peter Boghossian, a philosophy tutor and minor star of the New Atheist fraternity, has tweeted: 'Being published in the philosophy of religion should disqualify one from sitting at the adult table.'[1] The message is: being an intelligent individual and a person of faith are mutually exclusive.

This mean-spirited characterization of religious people is not universal across the spectrum, of course. Part of the joy of my job has been to meet many atheists who are lovely, open-hearted people who are delighted to engage in conversation. Nevertheless, the prominence of the New Atheism has led to a dramatic dip in the overall quality of conversation in both directions. If we aren't talking to one another any more, it means we stand little chance of understanding one another.

The Internet was supposed to change the world for the better. Here was a tool to open up a world of new possibilities and global harmony as it enabled the free flow of ideas on the information superhighway. But the main gateways of today's Internet, such as Facebook, Google and YouTube, have worked out that they achieve their best results (i.e. advertising revenue) by feeding people what they want to hear and watch in their news feeds. Rigged algorithms perpetuate a feedback loop – the right-winger only hears from those with the same views as himself; the radical feminist exists in an online world largely sympathetic to her own perspective. The same goes for the average religious or anti-religious web user. It allows people to live in an echo chamber where they can be protected from people who disagree with them.

The increasingly bipartisan nature of the online world tends to make the problem of having good conversations worse. Visit any Facebook group dedicated to discussing religion and you'll find things can get vitriolic very quickly. Many conversations descend into the equivalent of verbal hand grenades being lobbed over the barricades of our carefully erected worldviews.

Atheists attack 'faith-heads' while believers respond in kind by demonizing their opponents. It's not helped by the fact that online interactions are devoid of the tone, emotion and body language from which we take so many clues in our face-to-face conversations. A smiley 'emoticon' isn't quite the same as actually smiling at someone.

I'll begin this book by telling you how, by hosting the *Unbelievable?* radio show and podcast for over ten years, I've tried to reboot the concept of good conversations, and the effect it's had on me and those who listen in. In the process, I've aimed to put the God discussion back into the public sphere and get so-called opponents listening to each other again. There have even been some minds changed along the way, including mine.

In the following chapters, I'll be explaining what lessons I've learned about science, faith, philosophy and Scripture, and why I still find Christianity the most compelling explanation of the world we inhabit. Don't expect a comprehensive treatment of every sceptical question or disputed doctrine that exists. I won't be addressing questions around sexuality, the nature of the atonement, or which denomination you should belong to. Rather, I'll be seeking to defend the 'mere Christianity' of converts like C. S. Lewis and Alister McGrath. Is there a God? And if there is, why should I believe he has been revealed in the life, death and resurrection of Jesus Christ? If we can establish those core truths, then we can work the rest out later.

If you are a Christian reading this book, I hope it gives you the opportunity to examine your faith critically and the courage to share it with others confidently. If you are not a Christian, first, thank you for being open-minded enough to pick up this book. Second, I don't know whether you will be persuaded by what you read, but I hope it will at least give you a window into what I believe and why. And finally, whether you are Christian, atheist or something else altogether, I hope it gives you the desire to go and have a conversation with someone about it too because, as the ideas and debates in this book show, conversations really do matter.

1 Creating better conversations

It is better to debate a question without settling it than to settle a question without debating it.

Joseph Joubert

I grew up in a Christian family and attended church throughout my childhood. Like so many kids, Christianity was initially something inherited from my parents, but in my teenage years I had an experience of the love of God which transformed my faith from a general set of beliefs in God and Jesus into a living relationship.

Various people played a part in the events that led up to that conversion moment – a loving and wise youth pastor, peers in my youth group, my parents and friends at the Evangelical Charismatic church we were part of. But the experience itself was unique and not something I've ever been able to reproduce. In that moment, I knew that Jesus loved me, and I felt a new love for him myself. I felt the reality of the forgiveness of my past mistakes. Now I wanted to pray, read Scripture and worship him in a way I had never felt the desire for before. Now I wanted to commit my life to following Christ and discovering his purposes. I had been – to use the Charismatic parlance – filled with the Holy Spirit and born again. Whatever language you choose to use, something had changed inside the 15-year-old me and, although the shape of my Christian faith would grow, mature and develop in subsequent years, that first supernatural encounter would remain a defining moment.

As such my Christian faith was primarily founded on an experience I had on one particular evening at a youth retreat in Northamptonshire in 1995, when God showed up. I suspect that something similar is true for most people who call themselves Christians. It's not that they can necessarily pinpoint a 'moment of surrender' like mine, but their faith is nevertheless grounded in an experience of God's presence in their lives, perhaps in some emotionally tangible way, or simply as a deep-down 'knowing' that has been there as long as they can remember.

The problem is that this kind of faith is difficult to express to others whom you may want to share it with. Such an intense, personal experience is almost entirely subjective. It's not the kind of evidence that will necessarily convince the sceptical enquirer about the truth of Christianity. Most of my school friends, on becoming acquainted with the newly zealous version of me, had a reaction along the lines of, 'Well, that's nice for you, Justin . . .'

And of course, a one-off experience, no matter how profound, will not sustain an individual's faith indefinitely. I continued to be fed by other experiences, relationships, prayer and study. During a gap year, while working in Christian mission in Uganda, I saw how faith impacts the real world. The intellectual side of my personality was also racing to catch up with the spiritual encounters as I began to read books by a variety of Christian authors. My undergraduate years at Oxford University were an opportunity to spread my wings further still, getting involved in the Christian Union and heading up a Christian drama society.

University was also a time when doubt first made significant inroads on my young faith. There were plenty of sceptics on hand ready to question my faith, and after one particular encounter I spent a few days wondering if I really believed in God or Christianity at all. I can't remember exactly what brought me back – sometimes waves of doubt wash up and then recede again. Certainly, C. S. Lewis came to the rescue. Books like *Mere Christianity* and *Miracles* helped to affirm the rationality of Christian belief even if they couldn't answer all my questions. But the experience of genuinely wondering 'Is any of this really true?' was a valuable one, and it wouldn't be the last time I asked myself the question.

It was another Christian student called Lucy who was the greatest influence on my spiritual journey. We met towards the end of our second year at university as we were both involved in a student production of the musical *Guys and Dolls*. I was playing Harry the Horse, and she was applying my make-up. Romance blossomed, but from the outset our relationship was strained by the fact that we came from very different church backgrounds. My non-denominational-Evangelical-Charismatic leanings were strange and sometimes disturbing to Lucy. She had been raised in a more mainstream Nonconformist church setting and had never had a 'wham' moment like mine. God had always just 'been there' while she was growing up. At university, she didn't attend any of the big Evangelical student churches. Instead, she enjoyed the opportunity to experience a variety of churches throughout the town during her three years, including singing in the choir of her college chapel each week – about as 'high church' as you could get, compared to what I was used to.

Somehow we steered through the differences in our backgrounds and approach to faith. The lesson for me was learning to see God as present and active in traditions very different from my own. Lucy was studying theology with a view to entering ministry herself, and we had many conversations about our different approaches to God, spirituality and church. We grew towards one another in mutual understanding. She came to appreciate the dynamism and experiential aspects of the faith that I had grown up with. I came to understand the value of patterns of worship and prayer outside my own experience. We were also both able to experience contemplative and liturgical traditions that had shaped the pattern of worship for thousands of Christians down the centuries. We both came out of the process as more rounded people.

Oh . . . and reader, I married her.

The conversations we had then are part of what define the kind of Christian I am today. My sharp edges were knocked off by those formative experiences, and I came to see God and Christianity in terms that were broader than the limitations of my grand total of five years as a committed believer.

UNBELIEVABLE? IS BORN

In retrospect, such experiences and conversations were instrumental in preparing me for the role I have been engaged in for over ten years, hosting a radio show that brings together people of different opinions for dialogue and debate every week – opinions, dialogue and debate that have helped to form the very book you are holding in your hands.

I had begun working at Premier Christian Radio shortly after Lucy and I had returned from a post-university gap year. It was a career that neatly married two aspects of my personality. Broadcasting gave voice to my artistic and theatrical leanings, and the Christian ministry of the station allowed me to serve God in a very direct way.

The early days of my career were a learning curve. I went from being taught how to 'drive' a studio desk on the station's long-running daily breakfast show as sidekick to its veteran presenter John Pantry, to being trained on how to write a news story, create an audio feature and conduct a radio interview. In later years, I would also move into written journalism, becoming editor of the station's sister magazine *Premier Christianity*. But broadcast journalism was where I cut my teeth. Most importantly, I learned the art of connecting with the radio audience – especially when it came to hosting phone-ins.

Pinpointing the story angles that would grab the listeners' attention and participation was vital. Get it wrong and it would mean filling time while staring at a computer screen bereft of callers. Get it right and the phone lines on the studio screen would light up with people eager to have their say. I soon learned that one of the fastest ways to spark a response was to feature a voice that the average listener disagreed with, even if it was just my own, playing devil's advocate.

Soon enough I was given the opportunity to create a radio show for myself, from scratch. A weekly spot in the schedule that I could call my own. Premier Christian Radio was already very good at a specific sort of broadcasting. With a clear mandate to educate, encourage and entertain Christians across the UK with our programming, we were great at showcasing Christians on the radio talking to Christians at home about Christian things. All of which is important and helpful.

But I also wanted to widen the conversation. With less than 5 per cent of the UK attending church on Sunday, what about reaching the vast untapped non-Christian audience out there too? What if we tried talking to people outside our own bubble? The final format of the new show was fairly simple. I would sit down with two guests, one a Christian and the other not, to talk to them about why one believed and the other didn't. We would take calls from listeners and see what they had to say. And we would title the show *Unbelievable?*. The question mark was essential. Each show would debate a question, with the intention of testing the central claims of Christianity – could they stand up to scrutiny? What were the alternative views? And, along the way, what could we learn from inviting people outside the Christian faith into our big conversations?

On a Saturday afternoon in late November 2005 the first episode of *Unbelievable?* aired. There were no superstars of either the atheist or Christian variety to start with. My very first guests were an Anglican priest called John Twisleton and his non-believing neighbour Clive Boutle. They talked about their different journeys. Clive was happy to call himself an atheist but not of the fire-breathing sort. John was a model of civility and Christian witness but wouldn't have described himself as an 'apologetics expert'. But that was where we began. Two people describing why they did and didn't believe. Just one conversation, one idea, that would eventually lead to ten years of learning from each other.

All of a sudden, the calls came flooding in.

HOSTING THE CONVERSATIONS

As the show progressed over the following months, we began to cover specific issues: Is Scripture reliable? Why would God allow suffering? How do you explain the Trinity? At Christmas we asked if there was evidence for the virgin birth and at Easter debated the evidence for the resurrection. My book of contacts was beginning to fill up with people who were willing to come on the show and discuss these kinds of issues. And it wasn't just atheists and agnostics opposite the Christian guests. Hindus, Buddhists, Jews and those involved in esoteric New Age practices also featured on the show. Muslim guests would usually guarantee a lively debate and a big response from the listeners. There were memorable encounters between Jay Smith, a Christian missionary from the USA, and various Islamic apologists. Jay ran a ministry which regularly engaged in highly charged debates with young Muslims at Speaker's Corner in Hyde Park, and the conversation could get equally feisty when they came into the studio to have a debate with him. Not all the listeners enjoyed Jay's adversarial style. Perhaps, as Jay himself argued, their discomfort owed more to a Westernized view of how debate should be conducted. In contrast, Christian listeners from Africa and the Middle East were delighted at his willingness to stand toe to toe with his Islamic opponents.

As the show developed I also began to invite Christians of different theological persuasions for debate with each other. I tried not to do that too often, as I didn't want the show to revert to the Christian bubble I hoped to transcend. But such discussions were certainly useful for working out where I stood on important issues of Christian doctrine such as creation and evolution, how to interpret the Bible, and views of heaven and hell. Those are issues that frequently crop up in conversation with non-Christians too, so being able to parse the different views that exist was helpful as my own theology began to take shape.

Listeners would never quite know what to expect from week to week. Shows featuring academics could be relied upon to be well-argued, polite and safe. But those that featured opinionated guests and a zinging debate received the most feedback. I remember feeling sorry for the young biologist who was verbally dismantled in front of me by the journalist Peter Hitchens when they debated abortion. The outspoken Scottish Free Church minister David Robertson always generated a response too. Most atheists enjoyed crossing swords with him. Another left the studio muttering darkly 'Where did you get him from?'

Some shows were entirely unpredictable. I almost had to abandon a debate between Robert Spencer, a vociferous critic of Islam, and the Muslim apologist Adnan Rashid when they began trading insults. I paused the recording and in my firmest voice told them both to calm down or we'd be unable to continue.

Some of the most memorable encounters were with American megachurch pastors, albeit of very different kinds. In 2011, when Rob Bell's book *Love Wins* caused a theological stir with its apparent support of universalism (the view that all people will be saved), I invited him on to the show. We filmed a lively debate with Adrian Warnock, a more conservative Christian. The video went viral, introducing many new listeners to the show.[1] But when we filmed Bell two years later, shortly after he had endorsed gay marriage, he appeared terse and defensive in debate with the theologian Andrew Wilson. Unlike his previous encounter, I don't think he had come wanting to debate the subject, and the awkwardness of the exchange caught on camera was just as palpable in the studio.[2]

I also have the ability to upset megachurch pastors of the more conservative sort. A 2012 interview with the US church leader Mark Driscoll, in which he caused controversy by criticizing the quality of British preachers, led to him publicly attacking my journalistic integrity on his blog as well as questioning my theological credentials. I released the full recording of our interview online so that listeners could judge for themselves what had actually transpired, including the unforgettable experience of Driscoll turning the tables and grilling me on my doctrinal soundness.[3] It went on to become the most downloaded edition of the show, ever.

For the most part, however, the core of the show continued to be atheists and Christians getting together to talk. The show happened to be born just as the New Atheists were emerging as a force to be reckoned with. This was where the conversation stood between Christianity and the culture, so it was perhaps inevitable that *Unbelievable?* would primarily become a place of conversation between Christians and atheists. In 2006, less than a year after the show began, Richard Dawkins' bestselling book *The God Delusion* was published, and his name would crop up regularly on the programme over the following ten years. Eventually I was able to have the man himself on – but that's a story I'll save for later.

I'd like to tell you that *Unbelievable?* was warmly received from its inception by the listening radio audience, eager to hear Christians defending and promoting their faith as they crossed proverbial swords with their critics. But, if I'm honest, the show received a mixed reaction to begin with. Many Christian listeners did express delight that the show reached beyond the station's usual demographic and posed the kinds of questions they were encountering from sceptical friends and colleagues. Others were less convinced, pointing out that there were already plenty of atheists being broadcast on the BBC stations. Did we really need to hear them on Christian radio too?

I understood their concerns. You wouldn't normally expect to turn on a Christian radio station and hear an atheist making a sustained critique of some cherished Christian doctrine. As Veggie Tales creator Phil Vischer has said of *Unbelievable?*, it doesn't quite fit the 'safe for all the family' ethos of most US-based Christian radio stations. To his credit, Peter Kerridge, the station CEO, decided that the merits of the show outweighed any potential discomfort for some of the audience. The programme continued to be broadcast in its Saturday afternoon slot. Those who enjoyed it listened, and those who didn't learned to skip the 90-minute slot that the show occupied.

I knew the show wouldn't be everybody's cup of tea. *Unbelievable?* took listeners outside the Christian bubble, but many found it to be worth the risk. Bubbles are made for popping, and in our Internet age both believers and non-Christians are only a Google search away from radical scepticism about Christianity. If Christians want to reach out and share their faith, they need to be prepared for the arguments they will encounter. And on *Unbelievable?* at least, they got to hear both sides.

APOLO-WHAT?

From the outset, I intended *Unbelievable?* to be a place where, through friendly dialogue and debate, listeners would hear the rational case for Christianity. I had only been dimly aware of the word 'apologetics' when I began the programme. I was soon to learn that it was a word that neatly summarized much of what took place on the show. Rather than having anything to do with being sorry for something, it was based on the Greek term *apologia*, meaning 'to make a defence'. Christian apologetics may take the form of both defending the claims of Christianity and critiquing competing worldviews such as those of atheism, Islam and other religions. For a Christian, the core claims being defended include the existence of a Creator God, the reliability of the Scriptures, and the evidence for Jesus' life, especially his claims to divinity, and his death and resurrection.

Apologetics is an ancient branch of Christian theology and philosophy that goes back to the beginning of the Church. Paul was doing apologetics when he engaged in a debate with the Greek thinkers at the Areopagus in Athens in Acts chapter 17. Peter the apostle summed it up when he wrote, 'Always be prepared to give an answer to everyone who asks you to give the reason for the hope that you have' (1 Peter 3.15).

But modern apologetics has an image problem, often being viewed as the sole province of academics and intellectuals. Philosophical arguments for God and historical evidences for Christianity can be seen by the average Christian as an abstract exercise, too remote from the real-life world. As my colleague Jamie Cutteridge, editor of *Premier Youth and Children's Work* magazine, says only half-jokingly: 'I need an apologetic for apologetics.'

I hoped the show would take some of the best arguments for faith out of the ivory tower and make them more accessible to the Christians who listened. Inevitably, it was impossible to avoid intellectually dense material from time to time (though I didn't dare tackle the 'ontological argument' for God until nine years in). My job was to try to boil down the concepts as best as I could for the audience. It meant frequently asking my inter-viewees to reframe their concepts in simpler language, using ana-logies or illustration where possible, and explaining obscure terms (like 'ontological' – which, for the record, has to do with the nature of the existence of things, if that helps at all). Honestly, it was usually as much for my own benefit as for the listener's, helping me to wrap my mind around concepts in a 60-minute conversation that were often the work of a lifetime's study for those presenting them.

Church leader Tim Keller has described the gospel as the 'what' and apologetics as the 'why'.[4] It is aimed at showing sceptics that the claims of the Christian faith are worth their time and attention. Although I've always sought to create a fair playing field for apologetic debate, I'm also unashamed of my hope that *Unbelievable?* will spur sceptics towards taking the claims of Christianity seriously, and may even be part of their journey towards trusting Christ for themselves.

Because of the apologetics circles I tend to move in, I know of many people for whom the rational case for Christianity was a significant part of their journey towards faith. C. S. Lewis wrote: 'nearly everyone I know who has embraced Christianity in adult life has been influenced by what seemed to him to be at least a probable argument for theism.'[5] But for most Christians who (like me) embraced faith at an earlier stage in their lives, apologetics is often something discovered after conversion.

I didn't become a believer on the basis of a well-thought-out argument for faith. Rather, I had an experience that convinced me of the truth of Christianity. However, once that conviction had taken root, I was regularly challenged with reasons to doubt that experience and abandon my beliefs (not least in the afore-mentioned sceptical phase at university). This is when apologetics came into its own, providing objective evidence that confirmed the subjective experience of my encounter with God. Over time it became evident that the programme was scratching where many Christians were itching, as listening to the dialogues gave them the tools to engage their faith critically and the confidence to share it. The other demographic to begin tuning in were sceptics and atheists who enjoyed hearing their views being represented fairly and in turn were willing to hear the case for Christianity. But how did they discover a Christian radio show?

WHEN ATHEISTS LISTEN TO CHRISTIAN RADIO

As the show developed in its first years, it moved from a live format to a pre-recorded one. That meant I could no longer take listener calls to air, but had the advantage of focusing the show on a single topic (callers had a habit of diverting the conversation on to all kinds of interesting tangents). Feedback from listeners was still read out at the end of every show.

The engagement from the radio audience was going well, but I had a feeling that many more people, who couldn't be at their radio set on a Saturday afternoon, would be interested in hearing these discussions if we could make them more widely available. Before long, we began to post the audio of each show on the radio website and as a podcast on iTunes. And that's when things really took off.

Subscribing to a podcast is the modern equivalent of the 'appointment to listen' radio show or TV programme of yesteryear. I remember religiously sitting down with my sisters to watch the Australian soap opera *Neighbours* at 5.30 p.m. on BBC1 in the late 1980s, but the advent of catch-up TV has largely done away with the phenomenon. Now our appointments to listen are delivered at times convenient to us, wherever we happen to be. Once subscribed to a podcast, a listener's mobile device or tablet will be automatically updated when the latest episode is made available. Podcasting retains the immediacy and intimacy of radio but opens the opportunity up to anyone with a micro-phone, a laptop and an Internet connection.

What had at first been a show primarily centred on the UK began to acquire an increasingly transatlantic feel as podcast listeners in the USA, Canada, Australia and other countries around the world began to identify themselves. As the show gained prominence, so the number of people regularly downloading the show (and plundering its back catalogue too) continued to grow. At the last count, almost 2.5 million downloads of the show are being registered per annum.

Even more surprisingly, I began to receive many emails from non-Christians who had begun listening to the podcast. A frequent comment began to surface: 'You'd never normally catch me listening to Christian radio . . . but your show is the exception.'

As my knowledge of the Christian and atheist landscape grew, so I began to identify where the key battlegrounds lay in the debates and who the chief proponents were. I was able to secure some high-profile guests. Well-known Christian thinkers and philosophers such as William Lane Craig, John Lennox and Alister McGrath began to feature in conversation with atheist opponents. Whenever a significant individual with a large online following appeared, the show experienced a surge in downloads. So the weekly podcast audience gradually grew as new listeners discovered and then stuck with the programme.

This applied to the atheist community too. P. Z. Myers, a biology professor from Minnesota, runs 'Pharyngula', a blog that is popular with atheists of the more strident sort. Believers enter at their peril as the professor and his followers are not afraid to insult, ridicule and profane any Christian who falls in among the lions. Myers himself has courted controversy for stunts including the 'desecration' of a communion wafer pocketed from a Roman Catholic church. After he posted his own appearance on *Unbelievable?* to his well-read blog – an encounter with Christian geneticist Denis Alexander which turned out to be quite a good-natured discussion – I was immediately aware, from the feedback I began to receive, that a number of his atheist followers had turned their attention towards the show.

Other significant atheist guests would follow. From the USA: Lawrence Krauss a popular physicist, Michael Shermer the editor of *Skeptic* magazine, Eugenie Scott a well-known scientist, Richard Carrier a key name in the 'Jesus mythicism' movement, and many more. And there was plenty of homegrown British scepticism too. The Oxford chemist Peter Atkins, psychologist Susan Blackmore, children's author Philip Pullman, atheist philosophers such as A. C. Grayling and Michael Ruse, and stand-up comedians like Marcus Brigstocke and Robin Ince have all appeared over the years. There was the conversation with Derren Brown, the renowned British illusionist and mentalist, which you can read about in Chapter 6. Of course, the best-known atheist who has graced the show is Richard Dawkins. My two encounters with him and the atheism he represents are detailed in Chapter 9.

A number of live events also grew out of the weekly show. The annual *Unbelievable?* conference sees hundreds gather to hear from international Christian thinkers in what has grown to be one of the UK's largest apologetics conferences. I've also had the opportunity to host various public discussions between sceptics and Christians, including an event in California where I had the pleasure of meeting many Christian and non-Christian listeners from the growing audience for *Unbelievable?* in the USA. They repeated a frequent comment that I had heard from other transatlantic listeners: 'We don't have anything like this on our radio stations.'

A TWO-WAY CONVERSATION

I can't claim to have done anything spectacularly original in bringing together two different perspectives for a conversation each week. But in the present climate of argumentative and antagonistic debates (especially online), the sane, measured and usually friendly discussions I was hosting between intelligent people seemed to strike a chord with those discovering the show for the first time. That's not to say the sparks don't occasionally fly; after all, the programme thrives on the dynamic created by differences of opinion. Often there's value in hearing a conversation between guests who largely agree, but you can also learn a great deal from those who have a sharp disagreement too – and a bit of drama never hurts when it comes to good radio.

In moderating the discussions, I have largely tried to keep my own opinions out of the picture and let the guests do the talking. My job is to try to ask the questions that the listener, whether Christian or not, is asking. That might involve challenging a contributor to justify his or her claims, throwing in counter-examples or simply moving the conversation in a more fruitful direction once we've reached an impasse. If I'm contacted by listeners asking where I personally stand on an issue that's been under discussion, then I know I've done my job at maintaining a more or less neutral presence. Perhaps more surprising is when I'm contacted by people who, having listened to a few episodes of the show, reveal that they couldn't work out whether I was a Christian or not! I think that's a good thing. A moderator's neutrality gives both guests in the studio the confidence that they are being given an equal say, while listeners at home get to hear a fairly refereed match.

Of course, it's impossible to be completely unbiased, and I'm sure I've frustrated my atheist listeners on occasion by bringing my own Christian views into play. Not that I'm ashamed of doing so from time to time – it is a Christian radio station after all. Admittedly, no atheist on the show has yet been so struck by the dazzling arguments of the Christian guest that they've knelt down to make a tearful repentance live on air. I suspect that will probably never happen (although it would make for great radio). In reality, I don't expect a one-hour conversation to change the mind of those who come on to defend a particular view. However, the same is not true for those who listen. In my experience, there are many people who are quite open to changing their minds in the course of listening to argumentation and evidence. They are the people the programme primarily exists for. Debates are somewhat pointless if they merely reinforce each side's views. But good conversations have a habit of getting beyond the rhetoric and point scoring of a debate, and instead opening up a space for genuine learning. At its best, the show causes people to rethink their views and make room for new ways of understanding.

That means I've been privileged to hear all kinds of interesting stories as people have written in to describe their reasons for belief and doubt. I'm amazed at how many people are willing to share their entire life stories with me, someone they've never met, because they feel they know me after listening to my voice for so long. Often the emails are from Christians telling how the show has helped them approach difficult questions and strengthened their faith in the process. Others come from non-Christians who have been turned from hard-boiled sceptics into curious agnostics by the show, or have at least moderated their former view that Christianity is undiluted poppycock. For some, the show has been instrumental in a journey to Christian faith: people like Marc who wrote to tell me that he was as antagonistic an atheist as could be imagined, but that the show, combined with the influence of a loving pastor, had brought him to faith. He ended his message by saying: 'If your programme could reach someone as far gone as me, you're doing something right.'

However, since this is a programme that brings the two sides together, the traffic flows in both directions. There are many atheists and agnostics who write in to say that they are more convinced by the non-Christian speakers' arguments. I also receive messages from ex-Christians telling me that the show has confirmed their movement away from faith as they listened.

As someone who is an evangelist at heart, I'm naturally inclined to hope people move towards rather than away from Christianity when they listen, but I've never felt compelled to ensure that the traffic only flows in one direction. It would be impossible to host the free-flowing conversations that the show consists of and not expect people to make up their minds in different directions. Indeed, I never cease to be amazed at the opposite conclusions that different people often come to after hearing the same conversation.

Significantly, this is perhaps what differentiates *Unbelievable?* from many other worthwhile apologetics programmes that exist. The show does not deal in 'pat' or scripted arguments for Christian faith. There's a place for hearing a solely Christian viewpoint, but the cut and thrust of a discussion lets you hear what those arguments look and sound like with someone pushing back. And let me be honest: the Christian guests may not always acquit themselves terribly well. The atheists have the upper hand in some debates. That may just be the way the cards fell on that day. But this is the way conversation happens in the real world too, and I think there's immense value in hearing a real response from a real person.

I can't control how the debates will play out, but as a Christian I'm happy to do the best job I can in setting up the conversations and hosting them fairly. The rest I leave to the listeners to decide, believing that God is at work through the show, even when an atheist does a worryingly good job of putting his or her points across too! Yes, it may be less 'safe', but in an age of fake news, fake tans and even fake spirituality, people are looking for authentic conversations on faith, to help them make their own mind up. If you find yourself in that position too, then I hope the dialogue contained in the rest of this book will help you to listen, learn and dive into the conversation yourself.

SHAPED BY THE CONVERSATION

In the meantime, hosting the weekly programme has provided me with a ten-year course in theology and apologetics. To celebrate the tenth anniversary of the programme, I invited listeners to send in questions for me to answer. One of the most common was: 'Has the show made you change your own mind on any issues?' And more than once: 'How can you still remain a Christian having heard so many persuasive arguments from atheists and sceptics?' That's a fair question, and for an atheist for whom every argument against Christianity looks like a slam dunk, I can imagine that my persisting Christian faith looks like a wilful denial of the obvious. But as I've said already, two people can be listening to the same conversations for years on end and still reach very different conclusions, me included. Ten years on, I can honestly say that I am more confident in my Christian faith than when I began the show.

That is not to say my faith has remained unaffected over the course of the years. Numerous beliefs have been refined as I've grappled with the sweep of Scripture in all its variety. My views about hell and final judgement have changed; I've revised my understanding of creation and evolution; I think about human suffering and God's sovereignty differently now. I've had to confront perplexing questions that I hadn't even realized existed before I began hosting the show: how should Christians interpret the warfare passages in the Old Testament? Can we trust the accuracy of the New Testament accounts?

And yes, there have been a few periods of unsettling doubt for me when presented with cogent critiques of Christianity. There have been one or two sleepless nights along the way, as I battled to resolve a question that had been thrown up, especially when encountering certain objections for the first time. Not all of them have been resolved yet. There are plenty of issues that I've filed under 'to be decided', 'mystery' or 'I dunno'. I don't think doubt will ever evaporate, and why should it? We are rarely granted absolute proof of anything in life. Rather than seeing doubt as the enemy of faith, I've come to see it as an inevitable part of the process of making sense of our beliefs.

Yet there are ultimately only so many objections that can be levelled at Christian faith. After hearing many of them, I began to be able to categorize them mentally. I began to realize that they were often simply restatements of classic dilemmas such as the problem of evil, or revolved around a certain view of Scripture which wasn't necessarily essential for a solid Christian faith.

I don't consider myself to be a great theologian or defender of the faith, but being present for so many conversations has gradually given me the tools to sift arguments, sort the wheat from the chaff, consider the weaknesses in other worldviews and determine what seem to be the most significant arguments in support of Christianity. 'Iron sharpens iron' is a proverb often used by believers to describe the way they can benefit from mutual spiritual encouragement. But I have found the same applies when believers and non-believers dialogue. One's worldview may take a few knocks in the process but, if the conversation is entered into in the right frame of mind, a brittle faith can be tempered into an altogether tougher, sharper one in the end.

So, for the rest of this book, I'm doing something I don't normally do. Something I'm rather nervous about doing, if I'm honest. I'm taking off my neutral moderator's hat and telling you why I'm a Christian. You've already heard about the experience that led to my personal faith; now I'll try to explain the reasons why I think Christianity makes good sense objectively too. The next time someone asks me 'How come you still believe?' this is the book I will give that person. Of course, I'd still prefer to tell you in a conversation. But you're there and I'm here, so this will have to do for now. I don't claim to have all the answers, and I'm fully aware there are plenty of comebacks to the arguments I present, but this is where I stand now. After ten years of conversing with atheists and sceptics and hearing the strongest objections to God and faith, this is my case for Christianity.

2 God makes sense of human existence

The first gulp from the glass of natural sciences will turn you into an atheist, but at the bottom of the glass God is waiting for you.

Attributed to Werner Heisenberg

Few people in the world live in places which get truly dark. By 'dark', I mean the undiluted inky blackness of night. Electric illumination, with all its benefits, has also caused the modern phenomenon of light pollution. Towns and cities lighting up their streets and buildings cause such a glare that only the brightest stars in the night sky can be observed by the naked eye. Most of the majesty of the universe above us is obscured for the average observer, and even powerful telescopes struggle in the wrong conditions. This is not only true in the visible, but also in the radio regions of the light spectrum, making it difficult for radio telescopes to 'see' the sky. The only truly dark places on our earth where an undiluted night sky can be observed are now located far from urban centres.

One of those places is the Owens Valley in California. There, in the shadow of the Sierra mountains, the bowl-shaped dishes of Caltech's Radio Observatory point directly up to the night sky, receiving and filtering signals from distant parts of the universe.

One of the scientists who spent his early career analysing the data they receive is Dr David Rogstad.

The Milky Way galaxy that our solar system inhabits is a huge spiral, turning at 168 miles per second. Rogstad's research at Caltech has included determining the direction and speed of the spin of other galaxies across the universe by observing the type of radiation emitted by their neutral hydrogen dust clouds. But his skills were later employed at NASA's Caltech Jet Propulsion Laboratory to help save the Galileo space project from failure in the 1990s.

Galileo was an unmanned space probe launched in 1989 in order to reach its destination Jupiter in 1995, and tasked with recording important information about the planet and the solar system. But the mission almost failed because the craft's main antenna, which was supposed to transmit the data back to earth, did not open properly. Rogstad led a team who, working against the clock, were responsible for configuring an array of radio receivers on earth that could magnify and capture the feeble signal being emitted by Galileo's smaller antenna, allowing the project to succeed.

As a Christian, Rogstad sees no conflict between his science and his faith. The astronomer serves on the board of the science and faith research organization Reasons To Believe, and says his Christian convictions are confirmed by science. When I asked him to recount a personal story of the way his appreciation of the universe connects with his belief in God, he described walking by night on the road towards the Owens Valley Radio Observatory with the brilliance of the Milky Way above him: 'It's pitch black, and you can't even see your hand in front of you. But you have the glory of this creation in front of you, seeing the stars and the wonders of the heavens. I couldn't help but worship.'

David Rogstad's experience is echoed by many, not least another David who wrote Psalm 8 in the Old Testament. Three thousand years ago, in a world still unsullied by light pollution, he too would have been looking up at a sky bearing innumerable shining stars when he set down these words:

> When I consider your heavens,
> the work of your fingers,
> the moon and the stars,
> which you have set in place,
> what is mankind that you are mindful of them,
> human beings that you care for them?
>
> (Psalm 8.3–4)

King David's sense of insignificance in the face of the vastness of the cosmos is even more acute in an age when observations of the universe by modern science make us realize just how truly tiny humans and the 'pale blue dot' they live upon are in the grand scheme of things. Was this all really set up with humans in mind? Are we significant in this vast cosmos?

Read on in the psalm, and David's answer is 'yes'. Despite the vastness of the 'heavens' (the translation of a Hebrew word that was used to denote the sky, planets and stars), he declares of humans that God has 'made them a little lower than the angels and crowned them with glory and honour' (v. 5) with their calling to look after this corner of creation.

In a pre-scientific age, David's sense of the purpose of his place in the created order came not from a thorough knowledge of the nature of the universe, but from his belief that he was made in God's image. That same belief informed the wonder that David Rogstad experienced as he looked up at the night sky.

But not everyone shares that outlook.

SEARCHING FOR INTELLIGENCE

Rogstad told me the story of a PhD student whose research he was supervising at the observatory. The young man was fascinated by the prospect of discovering signs of life elsewhere in the universe, and would later work on the Search for Extraterrestrial Intelligence (SETI) programme. When the radio telescopes were not otherwise engaged, the student would point them at patches of the sky in search of frequencies that could be a telltale sign of advanced alien races broadcasting their presence to the rest of the universe. Rogstad once asked him if he had considered that the universe might in fact bear witness to an intelligence beyond itself. What if there was a Creator who had sent us signs of his presence? But the young scientist merely shrugged his shoulders. Despite his obsession with searching the universe for intelligence, the question of whether the universe itself might have an intelligence behind it did not appear to interest him.

The question has certainly always intrigued me. Like David the psalmist and David the scientist, I too have stared at a sky full of stars and wondered at my place within the vastness. Through the *Unbelievable?* show I have also met many current and ex-Christians who have faced major crises of faith because of a perceived conflict between science and the faith they grew up with. However, I never personally met any such conflict in my own fledgling Christian years. The church I called home never pressed a particular interpretation of Genesis upon me. At school, the question of whether science and God were compatible may have been covered in my religious education lessons but was never presented as a problem in the science lab.

I have only one clear recollection of a conversation on the subject, and it was with my dad who, having studied biochemistry at Oxford University and with a career in electronic engineering, seemed a good person to ask. As a Christian, what did he make of the early chapters of Genesis? He suggested that there were numerous ways of interpreting it, but that many took the creation story as more aimed at answering 'why?' rather than 'how?' questions – more to do with theology than biology. It seemed like a sensible approach, but I would end up revisiting the questions many times on *Unbelievable?* with people of different theological perspectives.

My dad also said something else. As a scientist he found it intriguing that the emergence of life on our planet seems to disobey one of the fundamental laws of nature. The second law of thermodynamics states that, when left to their own devices, all closed systems (such as our universe), will move towards increasing 'entropy' – the scientific word for disorder. As a gardener (not a hobby he's managed to pass on to me), he likened it to the fact that, if he were to leave his orderly flower beds alone for a few years, he would expect to see things a great deal more disordered, with weeds and brambles, when he returned. That's the way nature normally works. Yet the development of life on earth and the human species seems to contradict that principle. His knowledge of physics told him what the simple constituent elements and forces of the universe looked like. But his biochemistry had taught him just how complex and ordered life is in the cell. In the case of life, the direction of travel was from simplicity to increasing order and complexity. Our existence, he said, seems to be crying out for an explanation.

We are rarely granted absolute proof in any field of enquiry. Most of the time we all look at the same set of facts and ask 'What is the best explanation for them?' Sometimes we come to different conclusions, and that's when the fun starts.

Over the course of the following chapters, I will aim to show that God is a better explanation than atheism for multiple aspects of our human experience. In Chapter 3, I will argue that God is the best explanation of human value, and in Chapter 4 that he is the best explanation of human purpose. But in this chapter I will argue that God is the best explanation of human existence itself.

WHO HAS THE BEST EXPLANATION?

The question of whether we, as humans, have an explanation for our existence beyond the natural laws operating in the universe is very much alive (if you'll forgive the pun). We are pretty amazing when you think about it – living, conscious, intelligent beings capable of using our minds not only to create a home for ourselves on earth but to try to comprehend the mysteries of the vast universe we happen to find ourselves in. Is atheism the best worldview for explaining the processes that brought about the wonder that is you and me?

Atheism can be defined in different ways (an issue we'll return to in Chapter 9) but usually involves a denial of the existence of God. Most atheists don't believe any supernatural realm exists at all. I've certainly never met one who did. For them, the only realm we have evidence for is the natural, physical realm. On this worldview there is no purpose or transcendent mind shaping the forces and circumstances that brought about humanity. Many atheists, especially popularizers of science, subscribe to naturalism – the view that all that ultimately exists is matter and energy, interacting according to the blind forces of nature. When coupled with chance and long stretches of time, these forces can produce remarkably ordered physical, chemical and biological systems. Yet however much we humans and the world we inhabit may have the appearance of design, we are in fact the chance by-product of an unguided set of physical processes.

A competing view is theism, specifically of the Christian sort. On this view there is a supernatural dimension to life. Matter and energy are part of the story, but they don't constitute the fundamental reality. Humans are not accidental by-products of an otherwise uninterested universe. We are meant to be here. We are special. There is an ultimate creative and loving mind that we call 'God' who is behind the whole story. And eventually, on the Christian view, that God became personally involved with us humans, in the person of Jesus Christ.

Which version of reality is true? The atheist's naturalism or the Christian one? Could the universe itself contain the clues that tell us not just how, but why, we came to be? Could God be the best explanation for both the universe and us?

THE ARROW OF EVIDENCE

Many sceptics of Christianity exhibit outright hostility at the notion that God is involved in any such explanation. One of the most vehement detractors of the compatibility of faith and science is the US physicist Lawrence Krauss, the cosmologist equivalent of the biologist Richard Dawkins. When he appeared on *Unbelievable?* in 2013, he stated that: 'All the world's religions and scriptures are in complete disagreement with science, and it's inappropriate to argue otherwise.'[1] Krauss had agreed to come on my show by phone with Christian thinker John Lennox, a professor of mathematics at Oxford University. Krauss lived up to his bombastic reputation, frequently arguing, interrupting and contradicting Lennox. His mood probably wasn't helped by the fact that he was phoning in from a hotel room at midnight in the USA.

Krauss's view is that the advance of science over the centuries has eradicated the need for God as an explanation. The 'gaps' that God once occupied have been closed up by scientific explanations. It's a theme in biology that Dawkins is firmly subscribed to, believing that Darwin's evolutionary explanation of how the various species on earth arose by purely naturalistic means has dealt a deadly blow to the idea of a divine Creator. When it comes to God, both Krauss and Dawkins see the arrow of evidence moving away from theism towards atheism.

However, I have been struck by the way in which the story of the direction of travel of scientific enquiry, towards atheism and away from God, has often been overstated. What if, in many respects, the arrow is actually travelling in the other direction, especially when it comes to our understanding of the universe?

If it isn't clear already, I'm not a scientist, but years of hosting *Unbelievable?* has given me the privilege of learning from many scientists, both believers and non-Christians. Through them I've been exposed to at least three key fronts on which advances in our scientific knowledge seem to have opened up the possibility of design and purpose as an explanation rather than closed it down.

One of the most controversial is the concept of Intelligent Design (ID) in biological systems, especially the fantastically complex characteristics of DNA, which is the information storage mechanism for all living things. Whether such a coded language, which is a necessary precursor to evolution, could have arisen via an unguided process is the subject of much debate both within and outside the Christian community.

Some theistic attempts to marry science with arguments for design do fall foul of the 'god of the gaps' that Dawkins and Krauss are concerned about. These are the 'bad gaps' which science closes down as it advances. ID remains a scientific and theological hot potato, and is often accused of invoking a 'god of the gaps' way of thinking. While it makes for a fascinating discussion (one which is still very much a going concern in my opinion), I shall set aside the question of design in biology for the purposes of this chapter, and focus on the other two frontiers.

What if some gaps are, in fact, 'good gaps'? These are the ones that science opens up as it advances. Good gaps are not based on ignorance but stem from new scientific information that seems to point towards a design and purpose beyond the scope of science itself. What if, in the end, not all explanations are purely scientific?

The two other frontiers where science has opened rather than closed down the God question are Big Bang cosmology and the 'fine tuning' of the universe for life. I believe that these two scientific phenomena point towards rather than away from God. They provide fertile ground for building a case that it makes more sense to believe in a Creator behind the whole show than to believe there is nothing but chance and natural law in operation. So let's turn to them now.

THE BIG BANG

Travel back to the astronomical institutions of 100 years ago, and the predominant view, held by physicists such as Fred Hoyle, was a 'steady state' model of the universe. The universe was a vast, perhaps infinite, cosmos that had simply always been there. In a 1948 BBC radio debate, Bertrand Russell, the philosopher and foremost atheist of his generation, argued that the universe was a 'brute fact', saying 'I should say that the universe is just there, and that's all.'[2]

However, the assumption that the universe needed no explanation of its existence was thrown into question in the second half of the twentieth century. A radical theory had already been proposed by a Belgian priest called Georges Lemaître, a professor of physics. He suggested that the universe had not always been as vast as it is, and had in fact expanded to its present size from an incredibly small point in the distant past.

The theory divided physicists. Atheists such as Hoyle expressed concern at the potential theistic implications. It looked a lot as if Lemaître was describing a universe that had popped into existence, though the priest himself never sought to use his theory as a proof for God. Nevertheless, the question 'What caused the universe?' naturally arose.

Hoyle dismissively called it a 'Big Bang' theory – a phrase which stuck thereafter – and clung on to his 'steady state' theory until his death. But by the late 1960s, the vast majority of cosmologists had accepted some form of Big Bang theory. Lemaître's proposal had been confirmed by the observation of the 'cosmic microwave background' radiation, a form of light from an early stage in the universe's history when the cosmos was still in a dense, hot state. When astronomers accidentally stumbled upon it in 1964, it provided physical confirmation that, if you ran the clock backwards, you would find the universe shrinking down to an unfathomably tiny size in its earliest phase.

Leading physicists such as Stephen Hawking went on to develop theories which predicted that the universe began its expansion from an 'initial singularity', an infinitely small, dense and hot point, some 14 billion years ago, and that it has been expanding ever since. All the space, matter and energy that fills our universe − even time itself − has its origins in this moment in the past. Did this count as a beginning?

In 2003, physicists Arvind Borde, Alan Guth and Alex Vilenkin published a now widely accepted theory that any universe in a state of expansion could be traced back to a time boundary in the past. Many have taken this as scientific confirmation that the universe cannot be eternal, but did indeed 'come into existence' in the past. Others object that since the normal physics of space and time break down as we approach the tiny quantum world of the Big Bang itself, we are not justified in reaching any such conclusion. Even the paper's authors are split on the theorem's implications. Alan Guth has stated that the universe probably didn't have a beginning in the past but is very likely eternal.[3] Whereas Alex Vilenkin has stated: 'With the proof now in place, cosmologists can no longer hide behind the possibility of a past-eternal universe. There is no escape: they have to face the problem of a cosmic beginning.'[4]

WHO SET THINGS OFF?

For many Christians, the evidence is strong enough to mount an argument for God. William Lane Craig is a notable Christian philosopher who has regularly appeared on *Unbelievable?* and is known as a formidable proponent of arguments for God in public debates with atheists. His 'Kalam cosmological argument' (KCA) has become one of the best-known modern-day philosophical arguments for God. In addition to the scientific evidence for a beginning for the universe, Craig also argues that the concept of anything physically existing infinitely into the past is philosophically nonsensical. If our universe really did extend eternally into the past, we would never actually 'arrive' at the present moment.

In summary, the KCA states that if the universe had a beginning to its existence, and if everything that begins to exist has a cause (in our experience things don't pop into existence for no reason), then the universe too must have a cause. A compelling case can then be made for the nature of that cause. For time, space and matter to come into existence, the cause itself must be immaterial, timeless − and incredibly powerful. There's only one clear candidate for that job − God.

As you can imagine, these kinds of arguments are steeped in debate and have been tackled on the show numerous times. But before becoming too bogged down in the specifics, it's worth considering the wider picture. In the past 100 years, the progress of science has shown our universe to be more curious than anyone ever anticipated. Our entire universe was, very briefly, once the size of the room I am writing in, and a moment before that it was the size of a basketball, and a moment before that the size of a grape. And at the very earliest moment, it appears to have been something akin to 'nothing' at all. The door is always open to naturalistic theories that could explain this strange phenomenon, but the facts that we currently have in front of us also seem to accord very well with the long-standing Christian view of a God who created the universe *ex nihilo* – out of nothing.

On this last point the debate has been stirred up most recently by the aforementioned Lawrence Krauss. The atheist physicist has twice been a guest on the show to discuss his book *A Universe from Nothing*. In it he says that physics shows us that the universe does indeed come from nothing. There's no need for God to light any blue touchpaper; the universe pulled itself into existence by its own bootstraps. However, many have pointed out that Krauss's use of the term 'nothing' is highly debatable, and doesn't mean 'no-thing' in the literal sense but rather assumes some pre-existent quantum vacuum state from which the Big Bang emerged, which of course only shifts the question of a cause one step back. God doesn't seem to have been eliminated at all.

We'll return to the philosophical question of whether God is a satisfactory explanation as the cause of the universe a little later. But as it stands, science in the twentieth century saw a significant shift that looks very consistent with the claim that God was behind the creation of the universe, and inconsistent with the atheist who claims that the universe is simply a 'brute fact' with no explanation needed. Let's line up our next piece of evidence.

FINE TUNING

I have an atheist friend whose Facebook profile, under 'religious beliefs', states: 'I can hardly believe that I exist.' It's a good line, but also an ironic one. The fact is, by scientific standards, human existence is incredibly improbable.

One of the early revelations I experienced when hosting discussions between scientists was learning about the existence of the 'fine tuning' of our universe for life. Advances in cosmological science over the latter half of the twentieth century began to reveal that, when the universe began, the fundamental forces it was birthed with were apparently 'fine-tuned' to allow for the emergence of life.

Some 30 or so fundamental numbers, such as the force of gravity and the ratio of electrons to proton mass in the universe, are so exquisitely balanced that the tiniest fluctuation from their actual value would mean that a universe capable of producing life could simply not exist.

So did we just get lucky? To answer that question we have to try to get our heads around the numbers we are talking about. The odds of the finely tuned universe we live in coming about by chance are so unlikely that it's difficult to conceive of the astronomically large numbers involved.

Take the force of gravity. We're all reasonably familiar with the effects of gravity – it's the force that keeps our feet stuck to the earth, the same one that purportedly caused a falling apple to collide with Isaac Newton's head. Yet gravity is a curious sort of force.

First, it's very weak. Every atom in the universe exerts a gravitational pull on every other atom in the universe, but the strength of the force from an individual atom is extremely small. You may not feel that's the case when you trip up and land in a heap on the pavement, but that's only because you are feeling the combined force of every atom in the world below you pulling on your body. Second, although scientists can describe the effects of this force in amazing detail, enabling them to accurately predict the motions of the planets hundreds of years into the future, no scientist really knows what gravity actually is. How and why does it emanate from every object of any mass in the universe? It's a mystery. And here's another question: why does it take the very specific tiny value that it does?

This second question is what's at stake when it comes to fine tuning. Gravity acts as a universal superglue. It holds together planets, solar systems and galaxies. Were the force of gravity ever so slightly weaker than it is, the glue would become too weak, and no objects of any sort would be able to form. The universe would be a place where matter was distributed thinly across the entire cosmos, with no stars, planets or galaxies present for life to have a chance of developing on. If the force was ever so slightly stronger than it is, the glue would become too strong, and the universe would soon have collapsed back in on itself. The result again: no life.

So just how finely tuned is the force of gravity? How much wiggle room is there?

Science tells us that if it differed from its value by one part in 10^{60} then the universe as we know it would be unable to exist. For those unfamiliar with the scientific notation of numbers, 10^{60} is a '1' with 60 zeros after it. Written down numerically it would come out as 1 000,000,000,000,000,000,000,000,000,000, 000,000,000,000,000,000,000,000,000,000,000. Or written out in words: one trillion trillion trillion trillion trillion.

That's a very large number, and therefore a very tiny window within which the force of gravity could differ from its actual value and still produce a life-permitting universe. There's nothing about the force of gravity that suggests it had to be what it is – it could potentially have taken an entirely different value. So what are the chances of hitting that tiny life-permitting value by accident? How lucky would you have to be? Using a familiar way of looking at chance and odds may help. For my sake as much as yours, I'm going to try to keep the maths simple.

THE COSMIC DICE

Imagine you have a regular six-sided dice in your hand. (Yes, I know it should be 'die' but that always sounds odd to me.) Mathematically, if you roll the dice the chance of a 6 coming up is 1 in 6. That's not too bad. But what are the chances of rolling 6 twice in a row? Well, the odds get longer – it's 1 in 6 multiplied by 1 in 6; that's 1 in 36. So you'd have to be rather lucky to get two 6s in a row. Every time you add the chances of rolling another 6 in a row, the odds go up exponentially and it gets even more unlikely.

So what if you rolled your dice eighty times and every single time you got a 6? That's quite unlikely, but it's possible . . . right? In fact, the chances of rolling a 6 eighty times in a row are around 1 in 10^{60}, the same amount of wiggle room that the force of gravity has.

Just to put that in perspective: how long would you have to stand there rolling your dice for (allowing about five seconds per roll) before hitting a lucky streak and rolling eighty 6s in a row? I'll spare you yet another very long number, but on average you would have to stand there rolling your dice for trillions upon trillions upon trillions of years before hitting that winning streak of eighty throws of the number 6. That's a *long* time. By comparison (as we noted earlier), our universe has only been around for a relatively paltry 14 billion years.

Perhaps this helps us to see how vastly unlikely it is that the life-permitting value for the force of gravity could have been hit upon by chance. And that's only one of numerous finely tuned fundamental forces that our universe is dependent upon, many of them even more exquisitely balanced.

BUILDING BLOCKS AND THE EIFFEL TOWER

Perhaps the most impressive example of fine tuning is the initial low entropy distribution of mass and energy in the early universe necessary for life. 'What is that?' you may ask. Here's my attempt at a boiled-down explanation.

I have a toddler who enjoys playing with a large tub of wooden building blocks. More specifically, he enjoys knocking over the carefully constructed towers I create for him. When we get the blocks out, he likes me to pick up the tub and pour them out on to the floor. Whenever I do it, the blocks spread out in an untidy heap. The way the blocks are organized in the tub before I pour them out, as well as other factors such as the angle I tip them out, the surface they land on and the density of the air, determine what sort of heap will be created – sometimes it's a bit more of a pointy heap and sometimes they scatter more widely. But it's always a disorganized heap.

However, it's theoretically possible that there is some arrangement of blocks in the tub which, when poured out in the right way, after tumbling and colliding, would end up neatly stacking into a miniature replica of the Eiffel Tower. My 18-month-old son would be delighted to knock it over as soon as possible, but I would be flabbergasted. What are the chances of that?

In a far more precise way, in the earliest moments of our universe, all matter and energy was organized in an incredibly dense but very specific way, before it was flung out far and wide as the universe began its expansion. The vast majority of the ways that the matter could have been first organized would have produced a universe full of black holes, completely hostile to the possibility of life developing at any point in its future. That's the equivalent of the disorganized heap of blocks that falls out of my tub, every time. But, as it happens, the arrangement of the matter in the early universe was set up to go down the Eiffel Tower route. It was precisely arranged so that it distributed itself in a way that meant only a relatively small number of black holes could exist, allowing stars, galaxies and planets to form, and the opportunity for life to occur at some point.

The fine tuning required for the universe to have this characteristic is an incomprehensible 1 part in $10^{10(123)}$. When Robin Collins, a philosopher of science, appeared on *Unbelievable?* he described the nature of that number by saying: 'If you took a sheet of paper and filled it with zeros, then reproduced zeros on sheets of paper lined up across the entire universe, 15 billion light years across, that number would still be smaller than $10^{10(123)}$.'[5] Others have remarked that if you wrote a '1' and then placed a zero on every single fundamental particle in the entire universe, you would still be a long way short of the length of the number in question.

That the various physical forces and initial conditions of our universe are incredibly finely tuned to allow the formation of chemistry, stars, planets, galaxies and ultimately life to come into existence, is a fact rarely contested by physicists.

The physicist Paul Davies, who is himself an agnostic, has said: 'There is now broad agreement among physicists and cosmologists that the Universe is in several respects "fine-tuned" for life.'[6] Fred Hoyle, despite his atheism, famously wrote: 'A common sense interpretation of the facts suggests that a superintellect has monkeyed with physics, as well as with chemistry and biology, and that there are no blind forces worth speaking about in nature.'[7]

The question that remains is: why are things this way? Philosophers such as William Lane Craig have pointed out that there appear to be just three possible explanations: chance, physical necessity or design.

Chance seems to be ruled out by the probabilities involved. Physical necessity seems to be ruled out by the fact that there is no obvious reason why the forces and initial conditions could not have taken very different values. That only leaves design.

Let's return to those trillions of years of dice rolling. If you sat down in front of a friend and rolled the number 6 eighty times in a row, it's highly unlikely they'd say 'Well done – what a stroke of luck!' They'd think you had loaded the dice, or tricked them in some way. We should apply the same logic to the fine tuning of the universe. Someone's loaded the dice of gravity; someone clever has pre-organized the tub of blocks. There's a mind behind the whole show that intended for us to be here. God.

SOLVING THE FINE-TUNING MYSTERY

There have been a variety of responses to the argument from fine tuning. Here are a few of the most common, and my reasons for thinking they aren't valid objections.

1 LIFE ADAPTS TO WHATEVER UNIVERSE IT FINDS ITSELF IN

When listeners of *Unbelievable?* offer their responses to the fine-tuning argument, an analogy about puddles frequently crops up. Borrowed from the author Douglas Adams, it imagines a puddle looking at the hole it fills and saying to itself, 'Gosh, look how very fine-tuned this hole is for me.' Of course, the puddle is mistaken – the water it is composed of simply assumes the shape of the hole that it fills. The same is true of life in the universe, says the sceptic. If a different configuration of laws had occurred we might not be here, but life would have emerged in a different way, adapting to the nature of the universe it was presented with.

The problem with this objection is that, without a vast amount of fine tuning to begin with, you wouldn't even have the chemistry needed for life of any kind to develop in the universe. Even with the right conditions, the idea that 'life always finds a way' seems to be an unjustified article of faith. There are all kinds of further probability barriers that would need to be hurdled before we got to life developing.

2 IF IT WEREN'T FINE-TUNED, WE WOULDN'T BE HERE TO SEE IT

Another objection appeals to the 'weak anthropic principle'. The reasoning runs: 'It's very unremarkable that we find ourselves in a universe fine-tuned for life; after all it's the only kind of universe in which we can be around to observe.' This rather obvious insight seems to miss the point of fine tuning. The atheist philosopher Stephen Law has criticized the objection by invoking an illustration first employed by the philosopher John Leslie. He describes it as the equivalent of a blindfolded man standing before a highly trained firing squad, but every bullet managing to miss him. The man escapes with his life, but rather than wonder whether the miss was deliberately arranged, he shrugs his shoulders and says 'But their all missing is not amazing at all. It's wholly unremarkable. After all, had they not all missed, I would not be here to ponder my luck!'[8] That doesn't make any sense, says Law, and I agree. We can't wave off the fine tuning as inconsequential simply because we are here to observe it – our existence as observers is the very thing that needs explaining.

3 FINE-TUNED? WASTE OF SPACE, MORE LIKE

Yet another objection argues that we are too insignificant in size to be able to claim that this vast universe was fine-tuned for the tiny shred of life that clings to a piece of rock in a backwater of the Milky Way.

There are a few responses to this one. First, it can be argued that the size of our universe is itself a factor of the fine tuning. The carbon atoms that would eventually make up you and me were produced by reactions (which are also fine-tuned) at the core of burning stars. That means allowing a lot of time to pass, and the universe growing very large as it expanded. Second, it's worth noting that humans actually stand approximately midway between the very largest things (the observable universe) and the very smallest things (subatomic particles). It turns out we aren't so tiny and, in a manner of speaking, actually are at the centre of the universe after all. Finally, our 'pale blue dot' may indeed look insignificant in the vast expanse but, for the same reason my wife values the tiny rock on the band of her engagement ring far more than the large rocks piled in our garden, we know that size isn't everything, and I can imagine that God feels the same way.

THE MULTIVERSE

Perhaps the strongest objection to fine tuning is based on the idea of a multiverse. What if our universe is just one among a potentially infinite number of universes, each with its own sets of physical laws and conditions? The vast majority of those universes would be sterile, uninteresting places that are hostile to life. But we happen to have developed in one of the rare universes that has exactly the right physical laws and conditions for life. In a multiverse, it turns out there were trillions of opportunities to roll the dice after all − so our numbers were bound to come up eventually.

When I first came across the multiverse hypothesis, I was highly sceptical. It seemed like a convenient escape hatch for the sceptic, a speculative hypothesis advanced not on the basis of any scientific evidence but rather as a way to evade the force of the fine-tuning argument. As recently as July 2016 I stated as much in a video, saying: 'There's no scientific evidence for the multiverse.'[9]

Then Phil got in touch. Phil is an atheist show listener and keen skydiver who goes online under the name Skydive Phil. He's not a scientist but has taken a keen interest in these debates, producing a variety of videos interviewing physicists on the science involved. When I invited him on the show he argued, very convincingly, that the multiverse is not simply a flight of fancy to dodge the implications of fine tuning, but a valid prediction of inflationary theory. 'Inflation' here refers to the earliest nanosecond of the Big Bang, when physicists predict that the universe expanded at an exponential rate. Inflation solves a number of puzzles about the observable universe, but may also imply (for reasons frankly too technical to mention here) the possibility of a multiverse beyond our view. To hear Phil, in the company of the Christian astrophysicist Jeff Zweerink, explain how that could be, listen to the brain-melting edition of *Unbelievable?* entitled 'Who's Afraid of the Multiverse?', broadcast in September 2016.[10]

It was an important lesson for me in humility when it comes to overreaching in apologetics. On reflection I had overstated the case against the multiverse in that video. There are no guarantees that new scientific theories won't emerge that change our understanding of these issues again, and I hope I will always be open to revising my ideas in the light of new learning.

Nevertheless, Phil's intervention hasn't persuaded me that fine tuning is a dead end – far from it. The fact remains that multiverse theory is highly controversial within the scientific community. Any other purported universes are, and will always be, unobservable. They will always remain a prediction of a theory that can never be physically confirmed. For some in the field, this puts it beyond of the category of 'science' altogether. Others are reasonably sure that it's true. The Astronomer Royal Martin Rees is confident enough to bet his dog's life on it (which probably didn't go down well with animal lovers or the dog).

Others remain unsold on the idea. One of them is Australian astrophysicist Luke Barnes, whom I invited on to the show in a follow-up programme. He believes that multiverse theory is put into doubt by the possibility of so-called 'Boltzmann brains'. The bizarre hypothetical 'brains' in question are named after Austrian physicist Ludwig Boltzmann, whose ideas are behind the following counterintuitive theory.

If there were a multiverse containing many universes with different sets of values, the vast majority of which are hostile to producing life, then the most common type of observer for any universe to produce would be a 'brain' that randomly fluctuates into and out of existence in a small patch of order in an otherwise unordered universe. That may sound odd, but in a potentially infinite number of universes, strange things will happen sometimes, somewhere. In a multiverse, these types of disordered universes and their weird fluctuating-into-and-out-of-existence brains would significantly outnumber the sort of universe that we do in fact find ourselves in – a vastly ordered one observed by you and me with our human brains. But, since we aren't in fact a Boltzmann brain, we can conclude that there is probably no multiverse.

Furthermore, Barnes argued that, even if inflation produced a multiverse, the initial conditions for that inflationary period must themselves be very finely tuned. In other words, a multiverse needs fine tuning too, so you only push the problem one step back.

In the end, I've moved from being highly sceptical of the multiverse to – still quite sceptical. In this realm, all our arguments are by nature probabilistic so, while I can't be certain that the fine tuning is a result of a divine mind, it remains a strong contender. When I assess the evidence, the arrow still points towards a purpose and an intelligence behind the universe, one that fully intended for us to be considering these deep questions of science and reality.

SOMETHING RATHER THAN NOTHING

When John Lennox had his debate with Lawrence Krauss on *Unbelievable?*, the Christian mathematician said that he didn't believe in the 'God of the gaps' any more than his atheist opponent did.

But Lennox argued that God is a perfectly appropriate explanation when it comes to questions such as 'Why is there a universe to begin with?' When Krauss stated that the only valid questions were the 'how' questions answered by nature, Lennox responded:

> But that leaves completely untouched the 'why' questions. If you have a Ford motorcar engine sitting in front of you, you can ask the scientific question of how it works. But the 'why' question is still a real question. Why did it come to be? And the answer to that question must be in terms of a personal agent – Henry Ford. But that level of explanation doesn't conflict with the scientific explanation, because it's an explanation of a different kind.

Krauss, in typically ebullient style, responded by saying, 'There's so much wrong with that statement that it's hard to know where to begin. The "why" question is an invention. It assumes there must be purpose. But if there is no purpose the question is irrelevant.'

Lennox and Krauss disagreed fundamentally on whether 'why' questions which reach beyond the physical nature of the universe are relevant. Lennox sees God as a valid explanation in terms of a 'personal agent'. But others object to God as an explanation full stop. If the universe was created by God, then who created God? Why does God not require a cause for his existence?

One response is that if God requires a cause then we soon run up against the problem of an infinite regress of causes. Who created the God that created God, and so on? For anything at all to exist, it seems that you need the 'first cause' of an 'unmoved mover', which philosophers like Aristotle and Thomas Aquinas both argued for.

In the 1600s, long before the scientific evidence for a beginning of the universe came into view, Gottfried Leibniz advanced a cosmological argument from 'contingency'. When answering the question 'Why is there something rather than nothing?', he pointed out that there is nothing about our universe that suggests it *had to* exist; rather its existence is *contingent* (needs an explanation of its existence). But since the universe contains only contingent things, the cause must lie outside the universe and be caused by something that exists necessarily. God is a necessary being – his existence lies in his own nature rather than in any external cause. In that sense God is, by definition, the one 'uncreated' thing. The one thing that doesn't need a cause. That's not special pleading to treat God differently; it's just the nature of the kind of cause that we need to invoke in this case.

I've puzzled over these questions myself as they've been raised by both Christian and atheist debaters on the show. In doing so, I've been struck by the obvious yet remarkable fact that there is *anything* at all. It's something we hardly ever think about in the normal course of life. Like a fish in the sea who never once questions the reality of the water in which it lives and moves, we can be apt to miss the most obvious question of all: why does anything exist in the first place?

Like Leibniz, I can see that it's perfectly logically possible that there could have been nothing at all. And yet here we are. To respond that the universe, however it came about, simply exists as a 'brute fact' (as Bertrand Russell did in his day) seems to be an unjustified assertion. I find that God makes sense of the question of why there is anything at all, as well as the specific aspects of our universe that seem to be crying out for an explanation – its birth in the Big Bang and its remarkable fine tuning for life.

WHY CAN WE DO SCIENCE AT ALL?

There's one more tantalizing piece of evidence I want to lay on the table as we decide between atheistic and theistic explanations for why we humans exist in this universe. It's the fact that we can do science at all.

The only reason we can investigate the origins of our universe, and the forces it was birthed with, is because we are able to describe it so eloquently in the language of physics and mathematics. Most people (including the scientists who do the research) take this for granted, but again it's worth stepping back and asking 'Why should that be?' Why is our universe so eminently explorable? Why can a single human mind map it out with a pencil and paper? It's something that the physicist Eugene Wigner termed the 'unreasonable effectiveness of mathematics'.[11]

That the universe can be plotted in equations and numbers from beginning to end doesn't appear to be something that we as humans have 'invented'. Rather, the universe itself seems to be written in a mathematical language that we humans are uncannily adept at learning and utilizing to uncover the elegant matrix of our cosmos.

When the physicist and BBC radio presenter Jim Al-Khalili appeared on *Unbelievable?*, he admitted, 'It's a huge philosophical question: why does nature speak the language of mathematics?'

Al-Khalili is an atheist and a former president of the secular campaigning group the British Humanist Association. However, the broadcaster's own brand of non-belief is far less abrasive than that of some of his scientific colleagues. Whereas scientists like Krauss dismiss belief in God as 'intellectually lazy', Al-Khalili said: 'I'm not going to fall into that silly trap.' He takes the God question seriously.

On the show, he discussed the issue with theologian Alister McGrath, who pressed him on whether the existence of God could offer an explanation for our serendipitous universe. Al-Khalili responded:

> For me, not having an answer, not knowing, is fine. I would like to think I will find the answers. Who knows whether I will turn to religion later in life or have some epiphany? Maybe it comes down to what we as humans expect of how much we want to understand.[12]

Perhaps, then, it depends ultimately on what level of explanation we are willing to look for. There seems to be no intrinsic reason why the universe should be written in such laws and language, and present itself to us fertile for exploration and understanding. Despite Krauss's protestations, for most people the 'why' question is one that flows quite naturally from what we observe.

For those who want to ask 'Why?', atheism's only answer seems to be that it is a massive coincidence. But, on a Christian understanding, it tallies perfectly with what we would expect to find from a God of order and purpose who wants us to explore the universe we find ourselves in, and perhaps in the process see the Creator's own fingerprints embedded in the very fabric of physical reality.

After ten years of hosting *Unbelievable?*, I stand in far greater awe of the sweep of stars in the night sky and the fact that the universe they are part of sustains life in the form of you and me. In the past decade, science has often been the trump card played by New Atheists to show why religion has run its course. However, the real picture is not so simple, and I see all kinds of clues from science that point us towards rather than away from God.

So does science provide an iron-clad proof for God's existence? No. Could the scientific consensus change in the future? Of course it could. Is this all there is to say on the subject? Certainly not. The case for God is a cumulative one that reaches well beyond science alone, as we shall see in the next chapters. But on the balance of all the evidence I see so far, I cannot reconcile myself to believing that humanity is simply the accidental by-product of an undirected and unpurposed universe that came from nowhere and is heading into oblivion. I also can't escape a conviction that the order, elegance and majesty of the universe and our existence within it is crying out for an explanation beyond itself.

Atheism cannot account for such a world. That's why God is the best explanation for human existence.

3 God makes sense of human value

Nowadays people know the price of everything and the value of nothing.
Oscar Wilde

In the 1970s, Jaime Jaramillo, a wealthy businessman, was walking along the streets of Bogotá in Colombia when he saw a young girl climbing down through a manhole into the sewers below. Jaramillo went home, put on a wetsuit and followed the girl into the manhole. To his amazement he discovered about 90 children living underground in the filthy, rat-infested sewers.

They were the youngest victims of Colombia's so-called 'dirty war' in which government forces and paramilitary groups fought running battles across the country. In the social maelstrom, street kids found themselves at the bottom of the pile, often addicted to sniffing glue, involved in prostitution, and suffering from disease and malnutrition. The reason for their subterranean living space was that paramilitary gangs were killing the children who lived on the streets above.

Regarded as vermin, a gang member said of them: 'Killing these kids is like killing lice. We call them "the disposables".'

When a nine-year-old girl, Patricia Hilario da Silva, was gunned down in Brazil, a note was found pinned to her: 'I killed you because you didn't study and had no future.' She was murdered because, in the eyes of her assassin, she had no value, no usefulness to society.

Appalled at the situation in his home country, Jaramillo (or 'Papa Jaime' as he is affectionately known) went on to rescue as many kids from the sewers as possible, using his money to build a home where they receive an education and live in a loving Christian community. To date he has changed the lives of thousands of children.[1]

You probably find that story both inspiring and disturbing. We react with horror at the idea that humans, especially children, could be treated in such a way – as 'disposables'. But why exactly do we believe that human life should be valued? The killer's assessment of Patricia's circumstances was probably accurate, so why was the assassin wrong about the value that her life therefore possessed? And why, in contrast, did Jaime Jaramillo do the right thing – the humane thing?

To most right-thinking people these questions may seem obvious. Murdering innocent children is wicked, whereas helping them is good. Why are we even asking the question?

The reason we are asking is because that supposedly obvious truth evidently isn't obvious to everyone on the planet. So what reason would you give to the killer who judges another life worthless?

I find it very difficult to come up with a convincing answer on an atheistic worldview. There's nothing intrinsically special about us in a universe that is blindly obeying the laws of nature. There's no reason why humans should have any more claim for special regard on the biological tree of life than a louse.

Why then do we feel that view of humanity is so wrong? Why is it really, objectively, wrong to treat people that way? As a

Christian I have an answer readily available. I believe it's because we have the value of our Maker imprinted on us. Equally, the value of the rest of the living world is implicit in the role he hands his image-bearers of taking care of the earth. Genesis 1.27 affirms that God created humans 'in his own image'. And God was willing to take human form in the person of Jesus and give up his life for us. That gives humans enormous worth. A life valued by anything else – money, education, health, productivity – makes human worth a commodity and, in the end, makes some people disposable.

THE MORAL ARGUMENT

On 10 December 1948 the United Nations ratified the Universal Declaration of Human Rights, a document globally regarded as a milestone in world affairs. Its opening paragraph affirmed that 'recognition of the inherent dignity and of the equal and inalienable rights of all members of the human family is the foundation of freedom, justice and peace in the world'.[2]

The development of the concept of universal human rights is generally seen as one of the moral high points in the history of civilization. It is a declaration upheld by people of all faiths and none. Yet, as I aim to show in this chapter, the belief that humans are created free, equal and with inherent dignity only makes sense if there is a God.

In arguing that only God can ground the belief that humans have real, intrinsic worth, I will be developing a line of reasoning often called the 'moral argument'. It's a piece of evidence for God's existence that has often been debated on *Unbelievable?* and is one of my personal favourites. I find it very compelling, once properly understood. If you ever hear me overstepping my neutral moderator position and pressing the atheist guest more than usual, it's more than likely that we've been discussing this issue.

The argument is quite different in nature from the evidences we discussed in the previous chapter. Rather than appealing to aspects of the external world which seem to cry out for an explanation, we turn our gaze inwards and look at our own intuitions.

We all know that morality can vary a great deal between different people. You might think gambling is perfectly acceptable, whereas I may think it's an immoral waste of money. I may think paying for my child to attend a private school is my right, whereas you might think it an unfair use of privilege and wealth. I may be a pacifist, whereas you may say there are just reasons for taking up arms. There are plenty of grey areas when it comes to our ethics, and we are free to argue the pros and cons with one another.

For this reason, many people make the claim that morality is entirely 'subjective'. This means that there are no universal standards of good and evil, but that individuals decide for themselves what is right or wrong, depending on their cultural circumstances and personal point of view. They say that this shows why the moral zeitgeist of society changes over time as well. There are things that most people in the West are perfectly comfortable with today that would have once been considered scandalous by the majority of society, such as sex outside marriage. And there are things that were generally acceptable in the past that we may consider scandalous today, such as women not having the right to vote. As times change, so morality changes, goes the argument.

However, just as you and I may disagree over some moral issues, there are also some things which we probably *both* think are the correct way of acting, without exception. If someone falls over in the road, we should help them up and check they're all right. We should generally try to be honest, keep our word and act fairly. Showing generosity to others is better than being selfish. The list goes on.

There are also some things which I can almost guarantee that you and I *both* think are always wrong. For example, the abuse of little children. When I read horrific accounts of child abuse that crop up in the newspaper, it turns my stomach, not just because I am a parent myself, but because I cannot fathom how anyone could show such cruelty and depravity towards an innocent person.

These are the sorts of moral views that are relatively uncontroversial to most of us, and it is these moral beliefs that I believe we should classify as 'objectively true'. This isn't because we happen to agree on them – objective morality isn't decided on by a popularity poll. Rather these moral beliefs are objectively true because, when we look inside ourselves, we know that they *must always* be true.

Why? Well, anything less than an objective standard makes our moral beliefs a matter of opinion and feelings. So if a culture different from yours develops a practice, such as female genital mutilation (FGM), which you find abhorrent, you may object to what they do from your cultural perspective but, if morality is subjective, then in the end that's just the way you feel about it. What moral authority do you have to tell them that they are wrong? They simply have a different opinion from you. But, in fact, we both know that doesn't make any sense. If something is really wrong, then it's wrong for everyone.

In the same way that one plus one equals two, these are facts about the world. The abuse of women and children is always wrong – in all times and in all places. And the only way you can tell someone they *ought* to do something (such as end the practice of FGM or not abuse children) is if it's *really true*. Consequently, just as rational people ought to believe that one plus one equals two if they want their financial accounts to add up, so every rational person should recognize moral facts like the evil of child abuse, and our duty to act to stop it if we see it taking place.

IS RACISM EVER RIGHT?

Let's take the example of racism. If you travelled back to parts of the USA in the early 1950s, you would find a number of racist attitudes and practices that were generally accepted among the dominant population. A black person had to give up his or her seat for a white person on a bus. The black population did not have the same access to education and public services that the white population enjoyed. But just because that was the prevailing behaviour at the time – the subjective morality of its day – doesn't mean it was correct. The people who supported racism were in fact *wrong*, and those who led the fight against racism, such as Revd Martin Luther King Jr, were in the *right*. So my belief that racism is wrong can't just be a subjective result of a changing cultural zeitgeist. Rather there is a real objective fact of the matter that exists quite independently of anything else.

Every so often I get into a dispute on Twitter about these issues. It's a form of social media singularly unsuited for having discussions of any complexity, given its limit of 140 characters for messages. Nonetheless, when I do succumb to temptation and tangle with atheists on the rights and wrongs of religion, we often end up arguing about whether morality is objective or subjective.

I recently had a tweet-off with an atheist show listener who confirmed that all morality is subjective, describing it as 'a sliding scale'. So I asked what he thought of societies where racism was acceptable in the past. Was it OK to treat black people as second-class citizens in the American South when that was the moral fashion of that age? He said no, by responding that racism was wrong 'by definition', in the same way that a red flag is red. I couldn't understand how that was any different from saying racism is objectively wrong. The conversation didn't get very far.

So where is this leading and why is it a problem for an atheist worldview? If there is a realm of facts about moral values and duties, then we have to ask ourselves where that realm springs from. How can it be accounted for by an atheist? The only way we can speak of things being truly right and wrong is if there is a reality about these matters which stands apart from the material world. Our moral obligations are like a set of laws which have been determined in a separate domain. But determined by what? Laws don't just exist in a vacuum. Such a transcendent realm of moral law only makes sense in the context of a transcendent moral lawgiver. God.

THE GRIM REALITY

Many people who call themselves atheists may never have thought about the question of the nature of morality, and simply assume that their position makes sense. They may have a well-thought-out position on many ethical issues, and be willing to defend it if called to do so, but have never actually considered what their moral code is grounded on.

Most atheists I meet affirm some form of naturalism. Logically, their atheism commits them to the view that there is nothing more in the universe than the matter and energy that everything consists of. Consequently, the most that our moral beliefs can be are feelings, pressed upon us by our evolutionary history. So some people evolve a belief that racism is fine, while others evolve a belief that racism is wrong. However, these are merely opinions, useful perhaps for survival value, but there's no truth about the matter.

From a purely naturalistic viewpoint, we evolve whatever beliefs make sure we keep propagating the species. This means that any beliefs in the real existence of human rights, values and morality are ultimately an illusion. But, in my experience, most atheists don't like to admit the reality of this view when it gets spelled out in concrete examples.

I remember hosting a radio discussion hot on the heels of the launch of the UK 'atheist bus campaign' in 2008. This was a high-profile advertising campaign, crowdfunded by atheists, which took wings after Richard Dawkins threw his weight behind it. For a number of weeks, London buses bore posters with the words 'There's probably no God. Now stop worrying and enjoy your life.' The campaign was the brainchild of a young journalist called Ariane Sherine, who wanted to respond to the religious advertising she sometimes saw on London's transport system.

The campaign was a national talking point so I invited Sherine, along with other guests, to explain the motivation behind it. In the course of the show, she explained why, as a product of evolution, our morality changes over time, and that there's no need to be religious in order to lead a good and moral life. She spoke of her horror at acts of violence and oppression such as the rape of women in war-torn Darfur, Sudan. I didn't disagree with her at all. We could both agree that these acts are evil (though I couldn't help thinking that telling them 'There's probably no

God, so enjoy your life' probably wouldn't help much either). But I pressed her: did she concur with me that certain acts like rape are *absolutely* wrong, not just a matter of opinion or the social rules produced by evolution?

She responded that she was uncomfortable with speaking of absolutes; after all, there might be some gruesome examples where rape is justified for survival – a man in Darfur being forced by soldiers to rape his wife under threat of his entire family being shot, for instance. I pressed again: barring such instances, can we at least agree that rape *for the purposes of power* is absolutely wrong? Yes, she agreed *that* was wrong. Apparently conceding the point, she then asked me if we could move on, as it was an upsetting subject.[3]

It was grim stuff, admittedly, but it was a moment which exposed the problem for atheists who affirm the subjective nature of morality but then find themselves in a bind when it comes to truly horrendous acts. They don't just feel wrong. They *are* wrong. Period.

WHEN ATHEISTS CONVERT

There are of course atheists who have worked through the implications of their worldview and end up being unable to reconcile them to their innate belief that some things really are right and wrong.

C. S. Lewis's own journey from atheism to Christianity took place in two stages. First, he stopped being an atheist and became a theist. And then (through the influence of his friend J. R. R. Tolkien) he became a Christian. The first stage of the journey involved becoming convinced that a moral realm truly exists and so there must be more to life than a purely materialistic world. Ironically this realization stemmed from what most would consider to be an argument against God – the problem of evil. He famously wrote in *Mere Christianity*:

> My argument against God was that the universe seemed so cruel and unjust. But how had I got this idea of just and unjust? A man does not call a line crooked unless he has some idea of a straight line. What was I comparing the universe with when I called it unjust?[4]

Lewis's conversion was nearly 90 years ago, but the moral argument continues to influence people today.

In 2012, the mathematician and self-described 'geeky atheist' Leah Libresco appeared on *Unbelievable?* to discuss her conversion to Christianity. Up until that year Libresco had been a blogger of some repute on the atheist channel of the Patheos network, writing on mathematics and scepticism and interacting in a friendly way with many Christians. But the moral argument had niggled away at her for years.

She couldn't shake the belief that some things are really right and wrong, not just a product of her feelings and cultural preferences. Just as she recognized the reality of a mathematical realm that existed independently of us humans, so she had to admit the reality of a moral realm of good and evil.

When Libresco came on the show, I set her up in conversation with Hemant Mehta, a fellow blogger from the same atheist network she had once been part of. His blog is called 'The Friendly Atheist' and he was one of the first to post a critical response to the mathematician's conversion. For this encounter, Mehta was not so much 'friendly' as 'flummoxed'. He admitted that he couldn't even understand all her philosophical terminology, much less her line of reasoning. At points I wondered if I had mismatched my opponents when Mehta's responses to her explanations boiled down to 'I just don't get it'. Above all, he simply couldn't comprehend what it was about the moral argument that had possessed her to become a Christian (and even worse − a Catholic!).

As they went back and forth on the issues it emerged that Leah wasn't just won over to theism by the existence of objective moral values. She was also convinced by the fact that we, as humans, seem to have an uncanny access to this realm via our moral knowledge. Mehta holds that morality is just what we've worked out helps us get along in society, presumably as a result of evolution. However, Libresco argues that whatever role evolution had, we still believe we happen to have been delivered the 'correct' moral framework for humans. After all, among gorilla populations the practice of infanticide contributes to a stable society. If we'd been determined a different way by evolution, we might do the same. Was it just a massive stroke of good luck that we've instead evolved in a way that allows us to discover what's really good and evil? Again, her argument was that it makes more sense to believe in a God behind the process. It turned out that this undeniable moral realm Libresco believed in was not an inert and abstract one like mathematics. It forced itself on to her in the way she thought and behaved. This living law required a God behind it.

Overall it was an interaction that reminded me of the exchange in Acts 26 that took place between King Agrippa, governor Festus and the apostle Paul, who was brought before them as a prisoner. As Paul delivers his testimony, Festus exclaims: 'You are out of your mind, Paul! . . . Your great learning is driving you insane' (v. 24). Mehta sounded as confused by Libresco's conversion as Festus was by Paul's, but to me the mathematician's story is evidence that some roads to Christ involve profoundly intellectual journeys. While plenty of questions remained, Christianity could explain the things Libresco was sure of better than her atheism could. As she put it: 'Morality is something we discover like archaeologists, not something we build like architects. Christianity offered an explanation for it that was compelling.'[5]

The Christian thinker Ravi Zacharias tells the story of a sceptical student who approached him after a lecture, and insisted that there was no objective realm of good and evil. Ravi recounts the conversation, with other students looking on:

> I said 'Sir, I want to ask you a question. If I took a two-year-old child and put that child on this platform, and took a sword and cut that child up ruthlessly to bits, would you think I had done something wrong?' And he paused and he said to me, 'I would not like it, would not enjoy it, but I can't really say you would have done something wrong.' The people standing around were aghast. I said, 'My dear friend, even you, while denying the fact of evil and denying the face, the responsibility, of evil, find it inescapable to run from the feeling of evil.'[6]

The fact is that, deep down, most people do recognize the moral reality embedded in our universe that brought C. S. Lewis and Leah Libresco to a change of mind. That moral reality includes the beliefs that most people have about the inherent dignity of human life, which should be protected by a set of universal human rights. I fail to see how we make sense of that deep commitment to human value in the absence of a God who grounds the moral worldview we claim to be standing upon.

FIVE COMMON OBJECTIONS

Whenever we discuss these issues on the radio show, there are numerous objections levelled by the non-believer.

1 HOW DARE YOU! I LIVE A MORAL LIFE. I DON'T NEED TO BELIEVE IN GOD TO BE A GOOD PERSON.

I would agree entirely. And that's not the claim that I'm making – though people frequently think it is. I hope that nothing I've written so far suggests that atheists are immoral people who don't have a high view of human worth. Most atheists I meet are passionate about equality and justice, so of course you don't need to believe in God to be a moral person. The problem is that you can't make sense of those moral beliefs without there being a God.

It's also worth noting that you didn't get the values you espouse from your atheism. As a denial of belief in God, atheism is value-neutral. Even so, the abandonment of God in some societies has gone hand in hand with abandoning the distinctly Christian idea of the sanctity of human life. In its worst instances, this leads to Stalin's gulags and the killing fields of Cambodia. Atheists who lead a good moral life are normally a product of societies already shaped by centuries of Judeo-Christian morality.

2 THERE ARE PLENTY OF MORAL SYSTEMS AND PHILOSOPHIES OUT THERE. I CAN EASILY ADOPT A CODE OF ETHICS FROM THEM – I DON'T NEED GOD.

Like the previous one, this objection misses the point of the moral argument. You may well have struck upon a moral theory for the correct way to behave. That's great. But if you want those moral beliefs to be more than your personal opinion, and you think they should apply to other people as well as yourself, you can't escape the need for God. The moral argument is not about how you arrive at your moral beliefs, but how you ground them as true and binding for everybody.

3 THAT'S ALL VERY WELL, BUT HOW CAN YOUR GOD BE THE SOURCE OF MORALITY WHEN THE BIBLE IS SO FULL OF IMMORALITY?

This is a bit of a red herring. It changes the topic of conversation to a different subject − whether the Bible is a good source of moral teaching. There's nothing wrong with that question, and every Christian needs to consider how they should interpret the sweep of Scripture, including the hard parts of the Old Testament we normally skip over. But that's a separate debate.

The moral argument only deals with the beliefs you personally hold. You don't need to believe in the Bible to acknowledge that objective moral values exist, and require a moral lawgiver.

4 EVOLUTION DRIVES MORALITY. WE DEVELOP MORAL CODES BECAUSE SOCIETY FLOURISHES WHEN WE COOPERATE TOGETHER. IT'S GOT NOTHING TO DO WITH GOD.

This is the most common response I hear from my atheist friends. They deny the objectivity of moral values, explaining that they are merely a social framework for living that evolution has instilled in us. For example, the golden rule of 'Do unto others as you would have them do unto you' is manifested all over the world because people get on better together when they apply it.

But even if we accept this as a complete explanation of how morals arose (and I don't find it terribly convincing), it still leaves unanswered the question of why we should expect anyone to abide by them. The problem is that you can't get an 'ought' from an 'is'. Telling me *how* my morality came about doesn't tell me *why* I should therefore obey it. What makes a code of moral behaviour, such as the golden rule, binding on me or anybody else?

The answer usually comes back: because we build a better society that way.

But wait a minute – you've just neatly smuggled in the very thing we are debating. By talking about a 'better' society, or moral 'progress', or human 'flourishing', you have to assume there is an objective standard we are measuring things by or to which we are progressing. It turns out you do believe in objective morality after all.

5 ALL RIGHT, SMARTY PANTS, ANSWER ME THIS: IS SOMETHING GOOD BECAUSE GOD COMMANDS IT, OR DOES GOD COMMAND IT BECAUSE IT'S GOOD?

This objection is known as Euthyphro's Dilemma. If something is good simply because God commands it, that makes morality arbitrary. God could theoretically make anything good or evil. But if God commands something because he already knows it's good, then that makes God redundant – the moral value exists independently of him.

So are we caught on the horns of a dilemma? No, I think it's a false dichotomy. Philosophers such as William Lane Craig have offered a third option. Craig explains that 'God wills something because he is good. That is to say, it is God's own nature which determines what is the good.'[7] On that basis God's commands reflect his own nature of compassion, justice and love.

HUMANISM

Atheism has always had a bit of a PR problem when it comes to its own branding. The word 'atheist' is by definition a negative term describing what the individual does not believe in – namely, God. Christians, in this respect at least, have an advantage over their godless counterparts. Nobody wants to be forever defined by what they don't believe in, whereas the term 'Christian' positively invokes Jesus and what he stood for.

In response, various groups of atheists have adopted alternative, more positive terms to describe themselves. Some have been ill-judged: Richard Dawkins once coined the term 'Brights', apparently in order to distinguish atheists as intellectually superior. Even he probably now agrees that the term was patronizing at best.

A more positive-sounding label for atheists that has come into common parlance (and stuck) is 'humanist'. We started this chapter by asking what gives humans the inherent value that most people ascribe to them. As a Christian believes true value comes from being created in God's image, so a humanist believes that people create their own meaning and value, and don't need to look for answers beyond themselves. As the strapline of the British Humanist Association (BHA) puts it, humanism is 'for the one life we have'. As well as campaigning for a more secular society, the BHA offers trained celebrants for weddings, births and funerals; for people who want meaningful but religion-less rites of passage.

Some well-known personalities have officially embraced humanism. The comedian and composer Tim Minchin says: 'Having a non-superstitious worldview allows you to make more ethical choices based on a general desire to do the most possible good' and TV presenter Stephen Fry describes humanism as 'an acceptance of the awesome responsibility we each have for our own destinies, ethics and morals'.[8]

GOOD WITHOUT GOD?

Helping to give shape to this movement for ethically minded atheists is the philosopher Stephen Law, a regular guest on *Unbelievable?*. He wrote a book on humanism and is a member of the BHA Humanist Philosophers group. One of his appearances on the show was to debate the question 'Does Humanism Need God?' with Revd Angus Ritchie, who had recently written a paper on the subject for the Christian think tank Theos. Ritchie contended that atheists had unjustly appropriated the term 'humanism' for themselves when there is a long history of Christian humanism too.

Law said he was aware of the limitations that labels can create, and freely admitted that humanism has not always been the preserve of non-believers, but he maintained that today the term 'humanist' is primarily adopted by atheists. He said: 'Atheists who organize under that banner are adding a number of different conditions. They are requiring atheism or agnosticism, for example. That's the meaning that it has come to possess for those within that particular community.'[9]

He went on to say that our common human experience of a moral framework is not one that requires God as its author. Nor is the special status that most people ascribe to humanity explained by the Judeo-Christian belief in humans as image-bearers of God.

Law argued that God is too often invoked as a 'super-convenient form of explanation', justifying everything from the movement of the planets to changes in the weather. As scientific explanations have displaced these, so the need for God has diminished. The same applies to our beliefs about the moral values of humans, he claimed.

WHY ARE HUMANS SPECIAL?

But a tricky question remains. In 2002, at the fiftieth anniversary of the World Humanist Congress in Amsterdam, the gathered participants signed a declaration affirming 'the worth, dignity and autonomy of the individual and the right of every human being to the greatest possible freedom compatible with the rights of others'.[10] But why should humanists value humans so highly, and on what grounds should they treat themselves differently from any other part of the naturally evolved world?

This was the point that Angus Ritchie pressed, saying:

> Christianity provides the best foundations for most of the 'human values' in the Amsterdam Declaration. And Christianity provides much more secure foundations for humanist values than atheism does. So as well as arguing that Christians should be humanists, I argue that humanists should believe in Christianity.[11]

Surprisingly, Law admitted that humanists shouldn't necessarily be interested in singling out humans for special treatment:

> What matters about human beings is not the fact that they happen to belong to a particular species. If you asked most humanists what the relevant moral boundaries are, they'll say things like 'the capacity to suffer is a very important factor'. So, we shouldn't be causing unnecessary suffering. That is morally wrong.

This means that humanists should incorporate all kinds of species into their 'moral sphere', says Law, and in fact most humanists are more than prepared to do that. But then, what about the Amsterdam Declaration, which blatantly singles out humans for special treatment?

'I'm not comfortable about the Amsterdam Declaration,' said Law (he wasn't present at the event). 'If aliens turn up and show the relevant capacities and abilities to suffer, and all the other things we hold dear, then I would extend them the same moral consideration that I extend to humans.'

It's a sentiment shared by the Australian philosopher Peter Singer. He compares the privileging of humans over other animal species to racism, terming it 'speciesism'. What matters to Singer is 'personhood'. The capacity to reason, experience pleasure and pain, and have a desire to live are what should determine how many rights an individual has. This may mean that some highly developed animals qualify for similar rights to those of humans. More controversially he has suggested that newborn babies lack such 'personhood', and infanticide may be permissible in certain circumstances.

You may find that idea horrific. I certainly do. But it's also the chillingly logical conclusion of dispensing with the idea that human life is inherently valuable. The great irony is that humanism (in its atheistic form) doesn't in the end seem to have any obvious reason to be particularly concerned about humans. If the universe doesn't privilege one form of life over another, then why should we?

GOD IS THE BEST EXPLANATION

Yet we do privilege our own species above any other. Enshrined in our most important statements of universal human rights, we recognize the unique and fundamental dignity of humans, even down to the tiniest newborn baby. I suspect that, like me, you believe that an individual's value is not determined by his or her age, mental ability, skin colour, success, education, gender, sexuality or usefulness to society. And if we do begin to measure people in those ways, it is because we have abandoned the standard by which God measures them. Even glue-sniffing, sewer-living street children on the trash heap of life are loved by God, and they should be cherished by us.

I have tried to persuade you of two things in this chapter. First, that humans have a real inherent worth and dignity that transcends a purely evolutionary story of how morality came to be. Second, if humans have such value then it only makes sense if there is someone beyond nature who can assign them such value, the God who created them in his own image. I believe that the conclusion flows naturally once you have accepted the first premise – that humans are intrinsically bound to that objective moral realm of right and wrong.

Many people try to deny that premise, and theorize that we have merely been duped into an illusion of objective morality. But they never act like that in the real world. If they get mugged in the street, swindled in the shop or are treated unfairly at work, morality suddenly starts to look very objective and universally binding. When they walk out of their front door, they operate by the same principles of justice, compassion, right and wrong that we all do.

Atheism cannot account for such a world. That's why God is the best explanation for human value.

4 God makes sense of human purpose

He who has a why to live for can bear almost any how.
Friedrich Nietzsche

As any parent knows, the birth of a child is a life-changing event. Priorities, lifestyle and sleep patterns are all quickly rearranged to accommodate the now-most-important thing that has come into one's life. For some people, however, the change runs even deeper than that.

Jennifer Fulwiler grew up in a loving family, but one in which religion was painted as clearly false. Jennifer says that she never remembers a time when she believed in God as a child. Raised on a diet of 'science, reason and evidence-based rational thought', her bedtime reading was Carl Sagan's astronomy book *Cosmos*. From a young age, she knew that the world ran according to a well-established set of natural laws, and science was the de facto way of understanding everything. All the evidence confirmed that we live in a material world of matter, molecules, electrons and protons, with no need for God. Jennifer remained a happy atheist as an adult and into the early years of her marriage.

However, shortly after the birth of her first child, she experienced a dramatic shift in her thinking. Jennifer describes it this way:

> I looked down and thought: 'What is this baby?' And I
> thought 'Well, from a pure atheist, materialist perspective he
> is a randomly evolved collection of chemical reactions.' And
> I realized if that's true then all the love that I feel for him
> is nothing more than chemical reactions in our brain. And
> I looked down at him and I thought: 'That's not true. It's
> not the truth.'[1]

This moment was a turning point for the young mother, one
which would eventually lead her to Christian faith as described
in her book *Something Other Than God*.

Something had clicked for Jennifer. The scientific explanations she had grown up with weren't enough to explain the
totality of what she was experiencing in the bond with her child.
On a scientific level, she would have known well enough that, as
she looked at her baby, a whole bunch of neurons firing on
overdrive in her brain would be producing a set of chemical
reactions and hormones, and that those would be contributing to
the emotional urge to protect and care for her newborn son with
every ounce of her being. But that physical description alone
couldn't explain the actual experience of fully fledged love.

I can easily empathize with Jennifer's experience. With all
four of our children (yes, we're crazy), I've had the privilege of
sitting in a hospital delivery room, overwhelmed by the strength
of my feelings for the tiny pink bundle cradled in my arms for
the first time. I'm certain there's a very convincing evolutionary
explanation for why such feelings are produced within the parent
of any newborn child. But I'm also convinced that such an explanation doesn't describe the totality of that experience.

When I have sat in the early hours of the morning and
whispered prayers of thanks and love and hope for the future of

the child sleeping in my arms, I have a strong sense that I am doing more than simply obeying the hardwired instincts built into me by nature. What if the love I feel and the larger purpose I sense in that moment is in fact a reflection of something much bigger than biology?

If you are an atheist reading this, then your next thought is probably: 'Great! Here comes a logical argument for why we are more than matter, and why there's a purpose to life that transcends the physical. Let see what evidence Justin's got this time. Hopefully it'll be better than those last two chapters.' But my argument here is, in some ways, less 'logical' than what I've stated before. That's because when I argue that God is the best explanation for human purpose, I'm going to be appealing to a range of personal experiences and intuitions that many people claim to have, and looking for an explanation for them that cannot be contained within science.

EXPLAINING THE HUMAN SEARCH FOR PURPOSE

Our ideas about evidence and argument have been so shaped by modern rationalism that we tend to assume that our evidence for God must be similarly constructed. But God isn't an object you can examine in a test tube or analyse with statistical data (which is why I believe so-called 'studies' into the effects of prayer are fundamentally flawed). If God were that, then he would simply be another part of the natural order. But God, by definition, stands beyond the natural order. While science may give us pointers towards God, the raw data that brings most people to reconsider their atheism is not the kind of evidence that will submit to scientific analysis.

Irish rockers The Script made a similar point in their 2010 song 'Science and Faith'.[2] The lyrics speak of the fact that faith and hope can't be found by looking down the barrel of a telescope, nor will breaking everything down to the chemical level get you any closer to explaining love. It sounds even better when The Script sing it.

Rock bands don't sing about science very often, and if they do it's often to express similar sentiments to those of The Script – that science can't contain all the aspects of human experience. When a whole stadium at a Coldplay gig sings about the sky being full of stars and giving their hearts away, they aren't just singing about the wonder of the universe, grand as it is.[3] They are singing about how that wonder finds itself expressed in the reality of human love. Most of the songs ever written in the history of the world are human-centred songs about love, or losing love. They are about despair and hope, tragedy and triumph, losing your way and finding purpose.

According to Google, 'What is love?' was the most asked 'What is . . .?' question on the search engine in 2014, with five times more searches than 'What is science?' ('What is twerking?' came in at number seven).[4] Our common human experience throughout history has been the search for love, purpose and significance. Psychology shows that childhood experiences of love, and the affirmation of our significance and purpose, have huge ramifications for our future well-being. Searching for personal meaning and identity is the subject of the self-help volumes that line bookshop shelves and the magazines at the supermarket checkout. Many of them offer immediate solutions to our search for significance ('5 Steps to the Perfect Partner'), but the ache in the human heart yearns for more than temporary solutions.

Another popular Google question is 'Why am I here?' In typing that question, I suspect that users aren't searching for a birds-and-the-bees type of biological explanation. They are asking: if 80 years is my allotted span and then the lights go out, what was the point? Is there more to life than that? The same questions are at the heart of the book of Ecclesiastes in the Old Testament, when it states that God has 'set eternity in the human heart' (Ecclesiastes 3.11). The Bible claims that we are primed for purpose, and that seems to be borne out in our everyday experience.

Of course, my atheist friends will tell me that it's all perfectly explicable.

When I interviewed famed British illusionist Derren Brown about his loss of faith, he explained that we are biologically motivated to look for purpose where there really is none. During his Christian years he had believed in a divine purpose to life but now, as an atheist, had abandoned that idea for an evolutionary explanation. We are 'story-forming creatures', he said, who are prone to see ourselves within a grander narrative, because that's the way we get through life.

Philosophers such as Stephen Law will remind me about our ability to deceive ourselves into thinking there is purpose at work in the world. When our species lived on the savannah plains, we were always better off assuming that the rustling in the grass was a tiger waiting for us, rather than the wind blowing. But our 'hyperactive' instinct for agency detection also makes us believe in divine purpose. The long-awaited rain that falls is because God answered our prayer to save our crops.

I've even had atheists on the show tell me that any sense of personal self-determination is ultimately an illusion. The biological and physical forces that drive our lives are well beyond our control. In all, the message is loud and clear – there's no overarching story 'out there' to be discovered; the best we can hope for is to make the most of what we are given right now.

Richard Dawkins summed it up when he wrote: 'The universe we observe has precisely the properties we should expect if there is, at bottom, no design, no purpose, no evil, no good, nothing but blind, pitiless indifference.'[5] And I think that the explanations given by Dawkins, Derren Brown and the rest are true – if we assume there is no God.

If atheism is true then there is no ultimate right or wrong, there is no overarching narrative. Any sense of grand purpose is an illusion, and all human endeavours and self-made purposes will ultimately be gone and forgotten in the future. Science may tell us the extraordinary story of the beginning of the cosmos, but it also tells us the depressing reality of what the universe will be in the future. The sun will one day swallow up the earth and all its inhabitants, history and culture. But even if technology allows us to escape the planet, we can't put off our eventual annihilation for ever. As the universe continues to expand and its energy dissipates over trillions of years, all that will eventually be left is a cold, sterile void. There will be no memory of our brief existence on the pale blue dot we called home. There will be nothing of any interest at all.

But I see a very different universe from the one Dawkins sees. Where the atheist scientist sees only physical processes and laws that give rise to illusions of morality, purpose and free will, I see real beauty, truth, love, good and evil, purpose to life, freedom to choose and ultimate hope. I even believe that there will one day be a remaking of our reality, so that decay and death will no longer be the inevitable conclusion of our universe.

So have we arrived at an impasse? Why should I choose to believe that our drive to look for purpose is anything more than a predetermined evolutionary impulse? Is such a hope simply whistling in the wind as we head towards oblivion? Why is God a better explanation of our sense of human purpose than atheism?

C. S. LEWIS STRIKES AGAIN

You can probably tell by now that C. S. Lewis has been a major influence in my own journey of faith. It started early when my parents read me the Narnia stories (as I do now for my children). Then, at around the age of 11, I played the part of C. S. Lewis's stepson in a theatrical production of *Shadowlands*, the story of the Oxford don's relationship with the American poet Joy Gresham. One of the stranger experiences of my subsequent broadcasting career was being able to interview Douglas Gresham, the stepson I had played in my youth.

Later on in my adult years, I can think of several ways in which Lewis went on to inform my own understanding of why purpose and meaning in life can't be reduced to the physical processes of nature.

In the opening chapter, I described a period of doubt in my student life, and how Lewis came to the rescue. I distinctly remember the way Lewis's book *Miracles* helped to reframe the question of atheism. The second half of the book is his essay on why a purely materialistic understanding of our universe seems to derail the concept of reason. He explained how, if we are nothing more than the collision of atoms and electrons (albeit fantastically complicated), and all our thoughts and feelings can also be reduced to such physical events, then we run into a huge problem.

There's nothing 'true' or 'false' about the collision of atoms in the brain. They are what they are – physical events. Like the balls that collide with one another on a billiard-table, we have no personal control over these processes. So why should we believe that the thoughts produced by these physical events can be trusted?

Most atheists I know pride themselves on the use of reason and evidence in their arguments against God. But, on a purely naturalistic worldview, all that's *really* happening at a fundamental level is a variety of atoms bumping into other atoms, triggering electrochemical responses in the brain. What's more, because the universe runs on the strict principle of cause and effect, all those collisions were predetermined in the distant past. You and your beliefs are the product of a long chain of inevitable physical events.

So when you come to the conclusion that *there is no God*, that's just the way your brain happens to end up fizzing. And when I claim that *there is a God*, that's just the way my brain fizzes. But the atoms aren't doing any reasoning. It's all just a series of physical events – billiard balls bouncing off one another. They aren't the least bit interested in the truth or falsity of the thoughts they are producing.

As Lewis wrote:

> If minds are wholly dependent on brains, and brains on biochemistry, and biochemistry (in the long run) on the meaningless flux of the atoms, I cannot understand how the thought of those minds should have any more significance than the sound of the wind in the trees.[6]

So here's the problem. If this is a true description of how we come to believe things, then it radically undercuts itself. If our thoughts are determined by a non-rational process, then why should we trust the reasoning that brought us to believe in that very process? In doing so, the atheist has cut off the branch he or she was sitting on. The only way to guarantee that our reasoning is itself rational is if there is a mind beyond the physical stuff of nature.

Understanding the self-defeating nature of the naturalist worldview was a penny-dropping moment for me. It meant that seeking meaning of any sort was a self-defeating enterprise for a thoroughgoing atheist. Just as the collisions of the balls on the billiard-table only mean anything if there is a player who intended them to find the pocket, so we must be more than the matter that makes up our brain.

Let me extend my analogy a little further still. What about the game of billiards itself? Imagine if everyone came to the table with a new idea about how to play the game. One person thinks it's about keeping the balls in play for as long as possible without them going down the pockets. Another thinks the objective is to collect all the balls into one corner of the table. How would we decide what the game is for? The game only makes sense if someone created the rules for playing it, and if there is an eventual way of winning or losing. Perhaps, then, we shouldn't be surprised by the universal search among humans for a purpose and meaning to life in a world of competing options. What is the point of life beyond the everyday business of eating, sleeping and working until you die?

This second idea was developed in another line of reasoning by Lewis that has also resonated strongly with me. Termed the 'argument from desire', Lewis observes the common human experience of longing for something transcendent, and simply asks whether we should expect it to be fulfilled.

> A baby feels hunger: well, there is such a thing as food. A duckling wants to swim: well, there is such a thing as water. People feel sexual desire: well, there is such a thing as sex. If I find in myself a desire which no experience in this world can satisfy, the most probable explanation is that I was made for another world.[7]

It reminds me of a friend of mine who was one of the very first people I invited to talk about their unbelief in the early days of *Unbelievable?*. He has long been sceptical of organized religion but he adores classical music and feels something other-worldly when he listens. Acknowledging that many of the greatest works were penned by their composers to the glory of God, he once said to me, with a twinkle in his eye, 'Justin, when I listen to Bach, I am a Christian.'

Andy Bannister is a Christian apologist and gifted wordsmith. In his book *The Atheist Who Didn't Exist*, he explains why our transcendent experiences just don't seem to fit with the naturalistic atheist's account of reality:

> What was it that possessed evolution, normally so thrifty with its juggling of genes, to equip us and us alone among the animal kingdom with desires not just for cake and copulation, but for value, meaning, purpose, and significance? If atheism is true, we are at best biological freaks, whose desires no more map on to reality than do those of a dyslexic cartographer ... if atheism is true, not merely is there no meaning to which those desires connect, but the very fact that we have them at all would make us fundamentally irrational, poor, mad, deluded creatures. Evolution has sent us careering down a blind alley, even played a sick joke upon us.[8]

But I don't believe we're being deluded by our desires any more than the average atheist does. We all encounter transcendent moments – the soaring crescendo of a piece of music, watching a glorious sunset, holding a newborn baby. What if the meaning, purpose and desires we experience in those moments are not simply a tragically deceptive by-product of chemicals and atoms in their otherwise meaningless trajectories? What if we are feeling the echoes of beauty, meaning and joy that find their true home in the one who is the source of it all?

STOP WORRYING AND ENJOY YOUR LIFE

When the 'atheist bus campaign' was launched in London by the British Humanist Association, some commentators expressed surprise at the wording: 'There's probably no God. Now stop worrying and enjoy your life.' If atheists were confident enough to launch an advertising campaign, why not commit to 'There's *definitely* no God' rather than the tentative 'probably'? Whether it was a sense of humility or simply the restrictions of UK advertising rules, I think the wrong part of the sentence was being focused on. 'Stop worrying and enjoy your life' is the statement that most interested me.

The bus campaign also irked Francis Spufford, a celebrated writer whose book *Unapologetic: Why, Despite Everything, Christianity Can Still Make Surprising Emotional Sense* included the story of his journey from adolescent rejection of his Anglican upbringing back to Christian faith. For the reader who can cope with some bad language, it's as unconventional an apologetics book as you'll ever read. Delivered with a sharp dose of wit, it doesn't seek to make traditional arguments but aims to show why Christianity makes sense of our emotional needs as humans.

Referencing the 'enjoy your life' bus poster he writes: 'What it means if it's true, is that anyone who isn't enjoying themselves is entirely on their own . . . it amounts to a denial of hope or consolation.'[9]

When Spufford discussed the book on *Unbelievable?*, he described the New Atheist case against Christianity as 'absurdly time-lagged', saying:

> They assume that religion has precisely one piece of emotional content and it is fear, and the only thing that the thought of the existence of God could possibly hold out to anybody is a threat. It makes an irritatingly flat assumption about how human beings work. The idea is that, if you remove it, everybody bounds out into lovely happiness.[10]

I was able to pair him in conversation with the fantasy writer Philip Pullman whose His Dark Materials trilogy was widely touted as the atheist equivalent of the Chronicles of Narnia series. Their conversation was of the best sort between a Christian and an atheist, helped by the fact that both writers enormously respect each other's work. They had plenty to disagree about, of course, including the institution of the Church and the person of Jesus. But they both agreed on the facile nature of the bus campaign.

Given that Pullman is a distinguished patron of the British Humanist Association, I was surprised at how vociferous he was in joining Spufford to denounce it when he said:

> I thought that slogan was demeaning and stupid beyond words and I wish I'd had some say in it because I'd have said 'For God's sake don't do it! Say something else for goodness' sake; this is an absurd thing to say.'

Like Spufford and Pullman, I also felt that the campaign slogan represented a naïve form of humanistic optimism. It's the sort of 'brotherhood of man' sentimentalism that John Lennon promised in the song 'Imagine', if we would only dispense with the notion of heaven. But that theory was tried in some officially atheistic states in the twentieth century and the results were not pleasant. Abandoning God isn't a one-way ticket to utopia.

On a more practical level, what hope does the statement 'Stop worrying and enjoy your life' offer to the drug-addicted prostitute when it rolls past on a London bus? Or to the widow in sub-Saharan Africa who has lost her husband, children and livelihood to an AIDS epidemic? Stopping worrying and enjoying life may not be an option for them. For many people, God may represent the only possibility for a hope of ultimate redemption and justice in a world in which they drew the shortest of straws.

To this the atheist reply is often: 'I'm glad if you think that heaven offers some hope of an answer to the reality of misery on earth, but that's part of the problem with Christianity. It teaches people to put up with the world as it is on the promise of a better one to come.'

But the weight of evidence goes against that view. From its inception, Christianity has made social transformation a key part of its *raison d'être*. Heaven is not a place we are waiting to be evacuated to, but a redeemed and restored world that we work to bring into the present as we pray 'Thy kingdom come on earth as in heaven.'

The historian Tom Holland is well known for his popular accounts of the Greco-Roman world. Although he rejected faith in his youth, when he appeared on *Unbelievable?* to discuss how he changed his mind about Christian history, he described being stunned to learn of the way Christianity has shaped the modern world. His research had shown him how the concern for the poor and marginalized demonstrated by the first generations of Christians was unparalleled in the ancient world. The idea that human rights, welfare provision and equality will naturally prevail in any educated society was a secular myth, he said: 'Everything we take for granted as being part of the natural state of things absolutely isn't, and the reason we have these assumptions is because our society is saturated with Christian assumptions.'

His words reminded me (again) of C. S. Lewis, who responded to the charge that belief in heaven is a form of escapism by saying: 'If you read history, you will find that the Christians who did the most for the present world were just those who thought most of the next.'[11]

It remains true today. Critics may rail against the God who allows suffering and evil in the world, but if they go to the places where people are in the most need, they will invariably find Christians there toiling selflessly to feed the hungry, heal the sick and clothe the naked.

To be sure, both Christians and atheists are concerned with making the world a better place. But only one of the two works at it in the assurance that there will be a day when every wrong is righted and every tear wiped away. For the atheist, despite the sunny optimism of humanistic slogans, there is no such hope guaranteed. It may well be that the world remains a place of unmitigated injustice and sorrow until the human race becomes extinct. Despite John Lennon's words, history shows us that the march of secularism doesn't lead to a world in which humans will 'live as one'. The best that progress in the West offers many people today is shopping malls, reality TV,

Instagram selfies and blotting it all out on the weekend in an alcoholic haze.

Don't get me wrong. I'm not blaming the regression of Western civilization on atheists (and God knows the cancerous 'health and wealth' movement in the Church can contribute to the problem too). But I'm also convinced that a post-Christian culture has very little to offer people who are looking for purpose and meaning. We still experience that desire for something more than this world can give us, and certainly more than our celebrity-driven *X-Factor* culture is offering up. We are filled to the brim with entertainment and distractions but are starving for something that really satisfies. There must be more than this.

FINDING MEANING AS AN ATHEIST

Whenever the search for meaning is raised with an atheist on *Unbelievable?*, the frequent reply is that, in the absence of God, 'we have to make our own meaning'. This is usually cast as a positive thing compared to having meaning handed down from on high, but I think the problem of finding purpose in a godless universe is more acute than many modern-day atheists wish to admit.

In recent years, a number of non-believers have banded together to form the Sunday Assembly – a gathering frequently referred to as the 'atheist church'. On Sunday mornings, they find warmth, welcome and a sense of community in the company of like-minded sceptics. Instead of worship songs, they sing upbeat pop anthems like 'Don't Stop Me Now' by Queen, and in place of a sermon is a motivational talk on getting the most out of life. It's church but with all the spiritual stuff stripped out. Fronted by two stand-up comedians, it became an instant success after launching in London, and has been taken up in other countries (complete with church splits – some things never change).

When I interviewed co-founder Sanderson Jones, he was the embodiment of hopeful enthusiasm. He and the good folk at the Sunday Assembly represent the modern incarnation of optimistic humanism, and I respect their aim of finding inspiration and purpose together. But I suspect their meetings are unlikely to meditate too long upon the bleaker words of an older generation of atheists, such as Bertrand Russell:

> That Man is the product of causes that had no prevision of the end they were achieving; that his origin, his growth, his hopes and fears, his loves and his beliefs, are but the outcome of accidental collocations of atoms; that no fire, no heroism, no intensity of thought and feeling, can preserve individual life beyond the grave; that all the labours of the ages, all the devotion, all the inspiration, all the noonday brightness of human genius, are destined to extinction in the vast death of the solar system, and that the whole temple of Man's achievement must inevitably be buried beneath the debris of a universe in ruins – all these things, if not quite beyond dispute, are yet so nearly certain that no philosophy which rejects them can hope to stand. Only within the scaffolding of these truths, only on the firm foundation of unyielding despair, can the soul's habitation henceforth be safely built.[12]

It's not exactly the stuff of motivational car bumper stickers. So how do atheists deal with the existential reality of there being no meaning to life in any ultimate sense?

I always enjoy meeting sceptics on *Unbelievable?* but one of my favourite atheists by a country mile is Michael Ruse, a Brit who is Professor of Philosophy of Science at Florida State

University. Conversations with him are often punctuated by laughter, jovial ribbing of his theistic counterparts and a *joie de vivre* that many Christians could learn from.

But Ruse does not claim that atheism can provide 'meaning with a capital M', as he puts it. In a conversation with Andy Bannister, Ruse happily conceded that 'Christianity is a very serious answer to a very serious question' when it came to the search for meaning and why there is anything at all, even if he wasn't personally convinced by it.

Ruse, now in his seventies, confessed that he had half expected to find himself edging towards religion in his latter years, but that he hasn't required it in the end. An intellectually and emotionally fulfilled life has been enough. In a typically candid moment, he said:

> My mother died when I was 13. I feel for the first time in my life I could look her in the face and say 'Mum, I really think I have returned what you gave to me.' I have used my talents wisely (to quote the Bible). That for me is all-important.

Andy pushed back. What about people who don't have the opportunities afforded to him, a white, middle-class man, living in a prosperous Western country? Ruse admitted that there was no easy answer: 'I have nothing more to offer them than you do. I fully recognize that some people die early, that some people are born into situations that they can't pull themselves out of. These things just happen.'[13]

I appreciate the honesty Michael exhibits – that within his own fortunate sphere he can be satisfied with what he has achieved, but that atheism cannot offer any more than it claims to be. Things just happen.

So when atheists speak of the value of being able 'to make their own meaning', I am tempted to ask how we are to judge between the options on offer. How do we decide on how to play the game of billiards? In the lottery of life, different people may come to radically different conclusions about what their lives are meant for. One person may find fulfilment in giving up her life in sacrifice for the poor. For another, saving up for a comfortable retirement and golf every weekend may be the goal. Another person may find his meaning involves slipping into a state of numb bliss by injecting heroin into his veins every day.

How are we to judge between these different versions of meaning if there is no author of meaning to tell us what life is in fact about? And does it make any difference whether we judge them worthy or worthless since they will all be swallowed up in the void eventually?

When TV presenter Stephen Fry narrated a video advert for the British Humanist Association entitled 'How Can I Be Happy?', he described how every individual can find his or her own meaning. It may be 'walking in the woods, and caring for . . . grandchildren, or cooking, watching soap operas, and savouring a favourite wine or a new food'. The video concluded by advising: 'The time to be happy is now, and the way to find meaning in life is to get on and live it as fully and as well as we can.'[14]

I can agree with all that, and have no quarrel with those who find meaning in enjoyable pursuits. But I believe that the confidence in our own ability to live life 'fully and as well as we can' is misplaced. Call me a pessimist, but what happens when the things we have built our lives upon – family relationships, love of the arts, political activism, pursuing a successful career – are washed away by divorce, illness, failure, redundancy or death?

Jesus once told a story about two men, one who built a house on sand and one who built on rock. When the wind and rain came, the house built on sand collapsed. Jesus went on to claim that his life and teachings are the only thing upon which people can securely build anything. When Christians join their lives to his life, they are building upon the only solid source of security, identity and meaning that can stand eternally, no matter how hard the storms rain down. Generations of Christians who have faced poverty, failure, death and tragedy have found this to be true.

Jesus claimed to be the only one able to show people what life is really about when he said: 'I have come that they may have life, and have it to the full' (John 10.10). Yet this was a claim made by a man who would soon be tortured and crucified for the things he said and did, and a similar fate would await many of his followers. Bizarre as it may sound (and it sounded strange back then too), I believe that his death, offered on behalf of all creation, opened the floodgates to a new way of living. Those who have experienced its power claim that they have found the true life by giving their own lives away in his service.

This is the profound answer that Christianity offers to a world searching for personal meaning in self-help books, bus slogans, pop songs, atheist church services and videos about happiness. Only the author of life can hand you the key to unlocking life in all its fullness. And it starts by dying with him and being raised into a new way of living in which you realize that your life was never your own to begin with.

BATTER MY HEART

So here's the thing. I can make a rational argument that atheism is ill-equipped to provide hope and meaning. I can also claim that

God in Jesus Christ presents the fulfilment of all our searching for hope and meaning. But the only way I can justify that claim is to point you in the direction of people who have experienced it to be true. We will soon come to the case for the person of Jesus, his divine claims and resurrection. But finding true hope and purpose in him is not something I will be able to show you with a clever argument; it's a truth that each person must experience for themselves.

Yet I remain convinced that we see glimpses of that hope and purpose in the moments of transcendence that interrupt our lives and point us to God. Such moments were staging posts in the early life of C. S. Lewis as he struggled to make his atheism fit with his experience of 'joy' when he encountered poetry, literature, music and beauty that seemed to belong to another world, a process he describes in the memoir of his conversion, *Surprised by Joy*.

Holly Ordway also developed a love of literature and poetry as a child, devouring Lewis's Chronicles of Narnia series and Tolkien's *The Lord of the Rings*. Brought up in a secular home in the USA, she was oblivious to the Christian allegories in both. In retrospect, she believes that God was working through her imagination even as she dismissed the idea of religion as irrelevant.

As Holly progressed into higher education, her unbelief solidified into atheism, but when she began a career teaching literature and poetry she suddenly found herself undone by the power of what she was reading, especially within the Christian tradition. She described the experience to me:

> I remember reading the opening of John Donne's sonnet 'Batter my heart, three person'd God; for you as yet but knock, breathe, shine, and seek to mend.' I felt like I had

touched a live wire. That was the point at which the imagination that had been a river below the surface in me started bubbling up and I thought, 'There's something happening in this poetry, and I wonder what it is.'

Encounters like these brought her to the point of believing there was a God who fired the imaginative sense within her, but would eventually lead her also to investigate the beliefs of Christian poets such as Gerard Manley Hopkins and T. S. Eliot whose writing she connected with so profoundly.

> I had a two-step conversion, first to belief in God then to belief in Christ. If I hadn't become convinced that the resurrection was an event in history, I would have stayed a theist. So, I ended up becoming a Christian, as the imagination and the reason came together. I now see that what people like Gerard Manley Hopkins (hands down my favourite poet) gave me before I was a Christian was a little glimpse of the world that showed me that it made sense in some way that I hadn't experienced before. I've now stepped into that world.[15]

Having once experienced those stabs of joy, Holly went from appreciating the work of these poets to jumping into the same stream of reality they inhabited. This was the experience of C. S. Lewis too. In his little-known short essay 'Meditation in a Toolshed', he wrote about the difference between understanding something through observation and experience. The anthropologist who studies religion can give a compelling sociological explanation for why people believe, just as the biologist can give a chemical explanation for the love you feel towards your partner. Lewis likened this to standing in a dark toolshed and seeing a beam of light coming through the gap at the top of the door. This gives you an idea of what the beam of light is. But reposition yourself to stand looking along the beam of light, and the dark tool shed itself would disappear to be replaced by bright sun and the tops of the trees waving outside.

Lewis writes: 'You get one experience of a thing when you look along it and another when you look at it. Which is the "true" or "valid" experience? Which tells you most about the thing?'[16]

Holly borrowed Lewis's metaphor as we concluded our interview, saying of the Christian poets she had come to love: 'I've stepped into that "beam of light" so that I can look with them, and they can show me more than they could before.'

And so we arrive where we began. We are looking for the best explanation of things. Jennifer Fulwiler could not accept that her newly born child was nothing more than a complex set of chemical interactions, or that her own feelings of love could be accounted for that way. In poetry, Holly Ordway experienced a river of joy that she believed must have its source in something more than the material world. So we too must ask ourselves whether the common human longing for purpose and our experience of the transcendent can be fully explained by the unguided forces of physics and evolution which naturalistic atheism tells us is all that really exists.

Atheism and Christianity tell two very different stories. One is a story of ultimate purposelessness – the 'blind, pitiless indifference' of Richard Dawkins' universe. The other is a story of ultimate meaning and hope – hope that there is a reason for our existence, hope that our lives mean something, the hope that death is not the end. A hope that is expressed in the resurrection of Jesus Christ and which every Christian is called to embody in the real business of following him.

I have met many atheists in ten years of recording *Unbelievable?*. They are almost invariably intelligent and honest people. When I critique their worldview, I am not dismissing their own honest search for the truth. But we do see things very differently.

I find it very hard to believe that the rational and ordered universe we live in came from nowhere and is heading nowhere. I find it impossible to conceive that our intrinsic beliefs about human value are an illusion. Nor can I convince myself that our search for purpose and meaning are ultimately in vain. To me, it makes far more sense to read God's fingerprints and purposes both in the universe he created and in our human experience and longings.

These are the reasons that I believe God is the best explanation of human existence, value and purpose. But as long as these arguments remain words in a chapter of a book, we will only ever be staring at the beam of light. To experience the hope and purpose offered by God, we must look along the beam of light; we must risk stepping into the stream of faith.

When we do, I believe the human desire for 'more' is unequivocally answered in Christ. But why should you believe it? In the next chapters, I'll explain why I believe that the God who is revealed to us in human existence, value and purpose was most personally revealed in one human being – Jesus Christ.

5 Will the real Jesus please stand up?

I am an historian, I am not a believer, but I must confess as a historian that this penniless preacher from Nazareth is irrevocably the very centre of history.

H. G. Wells

You could almost hear the collective sigh of exasperation (heaved by a thousand Bible scholars) when Richard Dawkins tweeted a link to an article about Jesus to his thousands of Twitter followers in late 2013. Perhaps unsurprisingly, the arch-atheist turned out to be promoting a public event in London aimed at throwing doubt on Christianity. But this was more than your run-of-the-mill scepticism.

The speaker in question, self-published author Joseph Atwill, was due to present his thesis that Jesus Christ was a fictional character, invented by the Roman authorities to pacify the revolutionary sentiments of the Jewish people. His book *Caesar's Messiah* claimed that everything we thought we knew about Jesus and the rise of Christianity is a gigantic hoax, perpetrated by the Roman aristocracy. The fact that Atwill had neither scholarly credentials (he's a retired computer programmer) nor a jot of support from any academic in historical studies didn't seem to matter to a professor of zoology like Dawkins. After all, we all love a conspiracy theory, don't we? Especially when it comes to Jesus.

I remember when I received the email from Atwill's PR company detailing his 'explosive' theory on the non-existence of Jesus that would shake Western civilization to its core (presumably Dawkins received the same missive, sparking his tweet). Atwill was due to present his findings at a press conference which was being billed with all the historical intrigue of a plot from *The Da Vinci Code*.

But I didn't bother attending. I anticipated that Atwill would be touting the same kind of far-fetched conspiracy theories that I'd already run across a hundred times on the Internet. The only difference was that he had the money to publish a book, employ a publicity agency and rent a hall in central London. It turned out that the author's theory was regarded as way-out even within the 'Jesus mythicist' movement, a group considered left-field to begin with. Atwill was on the fringe of the fringe, apparently. Yet, for a day or two, his theory was splashed across several major newspapers and lent the backing of the world's best-known atheist.

Of course, you don't have to pay a PR company to get your ideas heard these days. The Internet will happily do it for you for free. Google can transport you to websites claiming to have irrefutable evidence that 9/11 was orchestrated by a shadowy cabal of powerful Jews, or that the Royal Family are shape-shifting reptiles from another planet, or that we've all been duped into believing the earth is round when it is in fact flat, or that the Holocaust never really took place.

The renewed popularity of bizarre conspiracy theories in our culture is a prime example of the 'post-truth' society we now inhabit. That's not a new word I just made up. In 2016, 'post-truth' was declared the International Word of the Year by Oxford Dictionaries, following a huge spike in the number of online articles that were either half-truths or patently false. The old adage that 'a lie can travel halfway around the world while the truth is putting on its shoes' has never been more true than in the age of the Internet.

Don't get me wrong, I love the web. We live with more information at our fingertips than we could possibly have imagined a few decades ago. But it also means we live with more misinformation than we've ever had to contend with before. The way-out can begin to look mainstream if enough people start sharing it on their Facebook feed. 'Jesus mythicism' is a defining example of that trend, and one we shall return to later in this chapter.

RELIGIOUS ROULETTE

In the previous chapters, I've outlined why I think God is the best explanation of various aspects of our universe and our experience as humans within it. In short, it makes sense to believe in God.

So the next obvious question that arises is: if there is a God, has he revealed himself to us? The Christian claim is that he has.

Jesus Christ was Yahweh in the flesh; the one human who lived on earth while uniquely sharing the divine nature of God. He was a Jewish man who, for the first 30 years of his life, lived and worked in an unremarkable corner of the Middle East that was under occupation by the Roman Empire. Then he began a three-year ministry of miracle-working and preaching as an itinerant rabbi supported by a ragtag group of fishermen, tax collectors and women followers. He declared that God's new kingdom was at hand and that he himself, as the promised Jewish Messiah, was the key to it. Ultimately, his words and actions brought him into conflict with the religious authorities in a series of events that would culminate in his execution on a Roman cross.

Christians claim that God came in Jesus, not only to show us what God is truly like, but in order that we might be reconciled back to that God through a defining act of sacrificial love, when he voluntarily gave up his life on the cross. Christians say he then rose again from death, vindicating his divine claims and inaugurating a new reality of resurrection life for every person who trusts in him.

That (in the briefest of nutshells) is the Christian story of how God chose to reveal himself. But, of course, there are many other options on the table too.

Islam, Hinduism, Buddhism and a plethora of other religions claim that they contain the true revelation about the nature of God and how he acts in the world. It could be that one of these is true instead. Or perhaps they are all false. For example, a 'deist' God may have chosen to keep himself at a cosmic arm's length from his creation, remaining a passive observer while humans run about squabbling over religion.

So how do we decide? Should we simply plump for one of them – like a religious version of a roulette wheel – and hope that we've landed on the correct option? I don't think we need to resort to that. Out of all the available alternatives, I think we have good reasons to opt for Christianity.

Some people will make their decision based on a personal experience that causes them to believe that Christianity is true, rather like the one I described of myself in the first chapter of this book. These accounts deserve to be taken seriously. If someone claims that his or her life has been dramatically changed through a spiritual encounter with Christ, supported by a radical change in that person's character, priorities and lifestyle, it counts as a form of evidence. Naturally the sceptic will be quick to point out that there are people of other religions who claim similar personal experiences. Granted. But that doesn't negate the fact that *something* has happened which requires an explanation, regardless of whether other people claim contrary experiences.

The other main way in which we can distinguish various religious claims is on the basis of historical evidence that is generally available. That could take a very long time, given how many religions there are in the world. But if Jesus was who he said he was, and if he miraculously rose from death to vindicate that claim, then we have a very strong case for believing that the Christian view is the true option over the other religious alternatives.

I have a set of similar-looking keys for the entrance door of the church where my wife is minister. Sometimes when entering the building I need to try a few of them in the door before I find the correct one. But if I find the correct one on my first attempt, I don't bother trying out all the others as well. Likewise, we aren't obliged to investigate exhaustively the truth or falsity of every religion if we find compelling reasons from the outset that Christianity is true. If God raised Jesus from the dead, then our search is over. We have found the key that unlocks the door.

Christianity makes a set of unique claims about Jesus. But it's instructive to note that the nature of the evidence for those claims is also unique among all the religions.

From its inception, Christianity has been a public religion making claims that could be held up to historical scrutiny in the place it was birthed. That's not true of other religions. The precepts of Buddhism originated in the mind of the Buddha alone. The ancient writings of Hinduism derive from mystical teachings that are not located in a historical framework. Islam is constituted by the teaching and stories of the Qur'an, as related to Muhammad in a private angelic visitation. Likewise, many newer religions have emerged out of the claims of private revelations to individuals. Mormonism and its founder Joseph Smith is an obvious example.

In contrast, the claims by the first Christians about the life, death and resurrection of Jesus are all events that were accessible in the public sphere, not the result of private dreams and revelations. From its birth, Christianity was an eminently falsifiable religion. That may sound like a bad thing, but in fact it's a very important principle in the search for truth. The claims of most religions simply can't be verified one way or the other. But we *can* come to a decision about Christianity based on the available evidence.

So what is the evidence for Christ? Can we trust the accounts of his life in the New Testament? How much can we really know about a man who lived, died and allegedly came back to life again 2,000 years ago?

REINVENTING JESUS

Jesus is, unquestionably, the most influential character in history, to the extent that we measure history in the epochs before and after his life. But the time gap since he lived has led to all kinds of conjecture about who he really was. Conjuring a Christ in our own image has become a common phenomenon. Believers of different stripes have variously cast him as a socialist revolutionary, a pacifist, or a Rambo-figure ready for a scrap with any liberal theologian who crosses his path. And there are plenty of non-Christian interpretations out there too.

In the past ten years of hosting *Unbelievable?*, I've come across a wide variety of people recasting the story of Jesus, but reinventing his character goes back much further than that. By the second century AD, various religious sects were writing their own accounts of the life of Christ that bore little connection to the testimony of the Gospels. The popular revival of interest in these so-called 'Gnostic' writings was led by Dan Brown, whose 2003 religious thriller *The Da Vinci Code* mixed fact and fiction together (and lo, 'faction' was born). Whether it was intended or not, the novel's runaway success led many of his readers to believe that the real history of Jesus had been covered up by sinister church bodies, a suspicion that has taken root in the wider culture too. Here are three recent popular theories about the 'real' Jesus.

1 JESUS THE GURU

Some authors have invented historically fanciful incarnations of Christ. One popular version has come from Deepak Chopra, a bestselling author of New Age self-help books. In *Jesus: A Story of Enlightenment*, Chopra imaginatively fills in 'the missing years' between Christ's childhood and his adult ministry. Drawing heavily on Eastern mysticism, Jesus finds spiritual enlightenment from a sage on an icy mountaintop before achieving 'oneness' with God.

Chris Sinkinson, lecturer at Moorlands theological college in the UK, is a regular Christian guest on *Unbelievable?*. As an archaeologist, he spends much of his time excavating the sites where Jesus and his contemporaries lived and walked. When I asked him about the New-Age-guru version of Jesus, he commented:

> Chopra's speculation on the 'God consciousness' of Jesus imports a very alien worldview into the Jewish-Hebrew context and culture of Jesus. This means his language is distorted completely. It's actually a very Gnostic view of Jesus – an anti-material view, which is not Jewish at all.
>
> Jesus draws attention to himself as the source of forgiveness, salvation and transformation. That makes him much more than just 'a great moral teacher'. In the end, Jesus wasn't crucified for being a New Age guru or teaching self-help therapy. Jesus was crucified for what was considered blasphemy among first-century Jews: his claim that as Messiah he was the one who could bring forgiveness and transformation.[1]

2 JESUS THE ZEALOT

A more serious attempt to reimagine Christ is *Zealot: The Life and Times of Jesus of Nazareth* by Reza Aslan. The book claims to show that Jesus was a rabble-rousing political revolutionary, not the peace-loving Messiah we thought he was. The author begins by quoting Matthew 10.34: 'I have not come to bring peace, but the sword.'[2] Aslan's Jesus becomes one of many apocalyptic preachers in first-century Judea, fomenting Jewish rebellion against the Roman overlords. Christ's crucifixion at the hands of the Roman Empire is at the centre of the book's thesis: it was a punishment reserved for criminals who had committed acts of treason against the state. Aslan claims that the early Church later refashioned Jesus as a peaceful spiritual teacher in the Gospels.

Aslan was brought to public attention after a Fox News interviewer questioned whether, as a Muslim, he had the authority to write such a book. Their toe-curling exchange, in which Aslan bristles with indignation, became a YouTube hit and contributed to the book becoming a bestseller. But when Aslan appeared on *Unbelievable?* to debate about the book, the interview felt no less awkward.

I had arranged for New Testament historian Anthony Le Donne to interact with him. Along with other historians, Le Donne had delivered a stinging rebuttal to Aslan's claims that Jesus was a political revolutionary. In a pointed article titled 'A Usually Happy Fellow Reviews Aslan's Zealot',[3] he accused the Iranian-born writer of recycling a long-debunked myth with shoddy scholarship to boot. Le Donne was no less pointed in the radio debate when he began by saying:

> Reading *Zealot* was a very troubling experience for me because there was an historical error on at least every third page. Even the 'sword' quote is immediately followed in Matthew by Jesus making it clear that he is referring to an inter-Jewish, inter-family conflict. Yet Aslan seems to suggest he is talking about a literal sword aimed outward to non-Jews.[4]

Normally, guests who join me manage to have a pleasant conversation, even if they disagree strongly. Not so in this case. Le Donne directly accused Aslan of being 'misleading', while the author shot back that Le Donne was part of a 'snobbish' elite of scholars who didn't like their views of Jesus being challenged. Who knew that New Testament history could be so exciting?

The debate may have been caustic, but most scholars in the field (and not just the Christian ones) felt the same way as Le

Donne. When weighed against the number of peaceful words and actions of Jesus, whose very death would come to represent a symbol of a non-violent response to power, Aslan's attempt to remould Jesus as a first-century Che Guevara seems stretched beyond credulity.

3 JESUS THE HUSBAND

In 2012, a different drama about the historical Jesus played out in headlines across the world: a newly discovered fragment of ancient manuscript in which Christ purportedly refers to his 'wife' was trumpeted as evidence that Jesus had been a married man. Throwing aside conventional academic etiquette, Harvard professor Karen King announced the news to the media before the scrap of papyrus had undergone scholarly review. Subsequent tests on the relic revealed the parchment was indeed old, but cast doubt on the text itself, which seemed likely to have been cut and pasted from an online document. King doggedly held on to her theory until she was forced to admit it was a forgery in 2016, following a riveting piece of investigative journalism by Ariel Sabar for *The Atlantic* magazine. He had managed to trace the provenance of the artefact to its original source – Walter Fritz, a dubious character with the means and the motive for creating the forgery.[5] King had been the victim of an elaborate hoax.

Anthony Le Donne's book *The Wife of Jesus: Ancient Texts and Modern Scandals* also examined the infamous Karen King manuscript as well as other historical claims that Jesus was married. After meticulous research, however, Le Donne arrived at the conclusion that Jesus was a celibate man, albeit unusually for a rabbi of his day. It's a non-sensational verdict which he freely admitted will not put him into competition with those whose book sales rely on more exotic theories.

'The old adage that "sex sells" remains true,' he said. He continued:

> If you put 'sex' and 'Jesus' in the same sentence, you are almost certain to get a headline. There is a pressure on scholars to go the sensationalist route. I knew that all I had to say was 'Jesus was probably married to Mary Magdalene or the woman considered to be a prostitute' for my book sales to go through the roof. However, I can't say that because it's not historically responsible.[6]

ELIMINATING JESUS

And that's where we come back to people like Joseph Atwill. The author's sensational claims about the non-existence of Jesus are the very antithesis of historical responsibility. Yet even though his theories are regarded as kooky even by his fellow mythicists, he and those like him are tapping into a general sense of distrust of the Bible that pervades our culture today.

Somehow, an assumption has developed in the public consciousness that the Gospels are a collection of legendary fables. A 2016 survey reported that 22 per cent of people in the UK think Jesus was a mythical figure, while 17 per cent are unsure whether he was real or not.[7] If accurate, this means that nearly 40 per cent of people doubt the existence of Jesus, a staggering indication of how pervasive such scepticism has become.

Part of the blame must lie with the Internet. Despite the fact that no widely respected historian holds to the mythicist position, if you type 'Did Jesus exist?' into a search engine you'd be forgiven for thinking that the issue is a seriously contested one. Sceptical websites and articles abound, the vast majority of which are run by atheists. Jesus mythicism is a classic example of a movement that can only exist online. Yet, for mainstream academics, the view that Jesus never existed belongs in the same category as those who claim that the moon landings were a hoax.

One such academic is agnostic Bible scholar Bart Ehrman. In years gone by, he won favour among the sceptical community for casting doubt upon aspects of the reliability of the Gospels. But when he wrote a book titled *Did Jesus Exist? The Historical Argument for Jesus of Nazareth*, refuting the idea that Jesus did not exist (because he kept hearing it from atheists), many of his former fans turned against him.

I invited Ehrman into my radio studio to explain why the atheist community remains so keen to fly in the face of accepted scholarship. He suggested that an anti-religious bias is clouding their judgement:

> My guess is that they are people who believe that organized religion is a major problem, so they choose to attack Christianity by claiming that it is rooted in a fairy tale. They can then claim that Christianity was something made up in order to oppress people.[8]

That interview with Ehrman was one among many I've had with him, but remains a memorable one, partly because it felt so unusual. Let me explain why.

Ehrman's own journey has involved moving from Evangelical Christianity to abandoning faith altogether after coming to doubt the truth of the Bible and the existence of God. I remember when I first came across his bestselling book *Misquoting Jesus*, in which he managed to turn the dry subject of textual transmission into a gripping account of why we can't necessarily trust the New Testament. Ehrman has mastered the art of making academic subjects accessible to a popular audience, and that particular book threw some serious doubts my way when I read it in preparation for interviewing him on my radio show.

In *Misquoting Jesus*, Ehrman explained how the original papyrus documents of the New Testament would have been long lost to posterity. He argued that the number of mistakes and insertions in the many copies produced thereafter cast doubt on the reliability of Scripture. By the time we came to record the radio show, my head was spinning with the new information I had encountered. How could we possibly trust the New Testament accounts?

On reflection that experience was a classic case of Proverbs 18.17: 'The one who states his case first seems right, until the other comes and examines him' (ESV). When Cambridge Bible scholar Peter J. Williams joined me in the studio to have a debate with Ehrman, it quickly became apparent that the 'problem' of the multiple copies of New Testament documents was also the solution.

For starters, it is precisely the fact we have so many existing copies of New Testament documents, both whole and fragmentary, that has allowed textual experts to compare and contrast variant documents in a detective-style process that recovers the original text. In a court of law, many witnesses to an event can build up a more trustworthy testimony to that event than a single witness, even if their accounts differ. Likewise, if we had only one surviving text we would have no discrepancies to worry about but little evidence of how closely it represents the original document. However, by examining the difference between the many existing documents available, we can deduce the correct words of the earliest texts, even though none of the originals survived.

Furthermore, when you drilled down to the number of passages actually thrown into question by Ehrman, it turned out that only a tiny handful of words were affected. What had initially seemed like a book that challenged the New Testament to its core turned out, on closer examination, to support the reliability of the vast majority of the text. It was an important lesson in withholding judgement until you've heard both sides of a case.

Over the years Ehrman has frequently returned to be a sceptical voice on the show, debating with scholars who affirm the reliability of the biblical record. In doing so, Ehrman has had precisely no vested interest in defending an orthodox Christian point of view. Which is why the conversation I had with him about those who deny the existence of Jesus was so unusual. Anybody tuning in to this particular episode could easily have mistaken him for the Christian apologist, so fervent was his critique of the mythicist movement.

The contrast of his position with the prevailing willingness to buy into a mythical Jesus was comically highlighted a few years earlier when Ehrman was interviewed on an edition of the *Infidel Guy Show*. As the title suggests, the podcast host Reginald Finley is an atheist, and appeared to have assumed that his guest, like him, was sympathetic to the mythicist view. Ehrman gave him very short shrift, pummelling him mercilessly with a variety of evidences for the existence of Jesus that left Finley slightly dazed. As a show host myself, it was the guiltiest of listening pleasures.

DOES MYTHICISM MAKE SENSE?

Although the established world of scholarship to which Ehrman belongs decries the rise of Jesus mythicism, the fact that so many atheists defend the view has led to several *Unbelievable?* debates on the subject over the years.

One of the most popular arguments (and the subject of a thousand atheist Internet memes) is that the Jesus of the Gospels is actually a pastiche of pagan deities who have similar dying-and-rising stories. The notorious conspiracy-theory film *Zeitgeist*, which has amassed millions of views online, makes exactly these sorts of claims. It includes parallels between Jesus and the Egyptian sky-god Horus, the details of whose birth and life supposedly line up with those of Christ.

For instance, did you know that Egyptians believed Horus was born of the virgin Isis-Meri (Mary) on 25 December in a manger/cave? That his birth was announced by a star in the east and attended by three wise men? That his earthly father was named Joseph and that he was of royal descent? That he was a child teacher in the Temple at the age of 12 and, at 30, he was baptized in the river Eridanus (Jordan) by 'Anup the Baptizer' (John the Baptist) who was later decapitated?

Gosh. It all sounds remarkably familiar, doesn't it? Maybe the Gospel writers really did pinch the Horus myth and turn it into one about Jesus?

Except they didn't. Because if you go and properly research the story of Horus rather than relying on the online articles peddling such claims, you'll find that none of the 'facts' I just listed are actually true. They are either completely fabricated, or versions of the Horus story twisted beyond recognition to create the parallels. In any case, the idea that observant first-century Jews would have been influenced enough by Egyptian pagan myths to invent a Jesus based on them is historically absurd. Yet, without fail, every Christmas a variety of

Horus-related Internet memes and articles pop up on my social media timeline.

To their credit, the most serious voices in mythicism have asked that we don't judge them by the standard of fanciful conspiracy films like *Zeitgeist* or the far-fetched conjectures of people like Joseph Atwill. I was often told by my atheist and Christian listeners that to hear the best case for a fictional Jesus, there was only one name I needed to invite on to the show: Richard Carrier. So I did.

Carrier is a leading (and sometimes controversial) figure within the global atheist community and regarded by many as the world's leading Jesus mythicist. Although he doesn't hold an academic post, he has a PhD in ancient history and describes himself as an 'independent scholar' whose research into the historicity of Jesus was crowdfunded by fellow atheists. So what's his theory?

In a nutshell, Carrier holds that early Christians believed in Jesus as a purely spiritual Messiah-figure who was located in a heavenly realm, and never walked the earth. In support of this, he points out that the earliest source of Christianity, St Paul (who did exist), never met a physical Jesus himself. Carrier believes the Gospels were later fabrications by Christians who wanted to flesh out an earthly story for Christ as their religion began to take shape.

If that sounds like an incredible claim to you, then you aren't alone. New Testament historian Mark Goodacre of Duke University expressed bafflement at Carrier's argument when they discussed it on the show. Goodacre described the 'strange leaps of logic' that are needed to eliminate a flesh-and-blood Jesus. He pointed out that the physical existence of Jesus is unquestionably assumed in a variety of ways throughout Scripture, especially in the earliest Christian writings we have, the letters of Paul.

For instance, in Galatians 1.18–19, Paul mentions James the brother of Jesus. It's a throwaway reference, but the fact is you can't be the brother of Jesus without there being a real Jesus to be the sibling of. Then there are the various references in Paul's letters to aspects of Jesus' earthly ministry, such as his summary of the Last Supper in 1 Corinthians 11 and Jesus' death and resurrection in 1 Corinthians 15. Nevertheless, Carrier insisted that all these references to Jesus can be recast as referring to a heavenly Jesus.

Mark Goodacre finished their interaction by saying:

> We create so many problems for ourselves if we take the historical Jesus out of the picture altogether. It's not just that we have Jesus' picture, but we have lots of other characters in the story too which only hyper-scepticism would cause us to doubt the historicity of.[9]

Hyper-scepticism is indeed the problem. For Carrier's position to be plausible, we must make a variety of assumptions. The Gospels must be the accretions of mythological stories, written well after the time they purport to describe. A whole host of characters, plotlines and detailed historical settings must be invented from scratch. The apostle Paul must be speaking in purely mystical terms when he makes references to the ministry of Jesus. It also assumes that all extra-biblical accounts of Jesus are simply trading off a pre-established Christian myth, or have been doctored by later Christians.

I don't often express incredulity on the show, but on this occasion I confessed to Carrier that I was having great difficulty buying his explanation. As Goodacre stated, the 'tortuous' explanations of the mythicists created many more problems than they solved. Like the theories of the 9/11 conspiracies or moon-landing hoaxers, I felt that I was being asked to swallow an entire alternative hyper-sceptical worldview along with Carrier's theory. Maybe he would tell me I just couldn't stomach it, but having met the world's most qualified mythicist, I was genuinely nonplussed by his theory and left wondering, 'Is that really all they have?'

So, colour me unimpressed. On the contrary, when it comes to historical evidence for characters from antiquity, I believe the life and death of Jesus of Nazareth is among the best attested of all.

THE EVIDENCE FOR JESUS

The four Gospel accounts of Jesus in the New Testament are estimated to have been written down between 35 and 65 years after his life. Mark is recognized as the earliest Gospel, written within the lifetime of Jesus' first followers, and John the latest. We have thousands of manuscripts of these Gospels from various centuries. Until recently, the earliest existing copies dated to around AD 100–150.

Recently, fragments of what are believed to be a copy of the Gospel of Mark were discovered in an Egyptian death mask and have been dated to the late first century. If the find is verified, it will be further confirmation of the close proximity of Mark's account of Jesus' life to the events it describes. Paul's letters were written even closer to the life of Jesus. Some traditions he quotes refer to creeds that were probably being recited by Jesus' followers within a few years of his death and resurrection.

Why am I telling you all this? Because, contrary to popular assumptions, the number and nature of the historical documents for the life of Jesus is extraordinarily strong compared to other historical figures of the time. A key principle in historical research is that the closer the written sources are to the events they describe, and the more of them we have to compare, the better their reliability. For many key figures of the ancient world, we have as few as 20 existing copies of the documents that detail their lives, often written down decades or even centuries after the events. This means, for example, that we have far better historical evidence for the life of Jesus than we do for the crossing of the Rubicon by Caesar, a major event in the history of the Roman Empire, which nobody questions. The crossing of the Rubicon has only four ancient authors who mention it within a relatively recent time of the event, writing within 65–165 years of the crossing. In contrast, the strong consensus of New Testament scholars today is that our four canonical Gospels were written between 35 and 65 years after the life of Jesus. And, as already noted, Paul provides even earlier data about Jesus.

It's also worth remembering that, within his own lifetime as a Jewish preacher in a remote province of the Roman Empire, Jesus was unknown on the world stage. The histories that tend to be recorded are of world leaders whose names appeared on the currency of the day or are engraved on stone tributes – the kind of artefacts which endure far longer than papyrus scrolls. Lesser figures didn't get their histories written down in ways that survived, if at all. So having *any* evidence at all for the life of Jesus is a minor miracle in itself.

As Goodacre noted in the debate with Carrier: 'The evidence we would expect to find is exactly what we do find – Jesus surviving in the memories of those who were closest to him.' The fact we have so many early physical records of his words and actions, unmatched by those representing more senior figures of his day, is remarkable.

But, however early historians may date them, can we trust these accounts? A frequent charge brought against the Gospels and epistles is that they were written by biased Christians, calling into question their reliability as historical sources. This has created a situation where some people seem to believe that nothing in the New Testament is admissible as evidence for Jesus. When Kenneth Humphreys, an enthusiastic popularizer of mythicism in the UK, appeared on *Unbelievable?* with Christian apologist Sean McDowell, he persistently refused to countenance any evidence from McDowell that was associated with Christians. It quickly became a frustratingly circular conversation.

With due respect to Humphreys, his demands amount to a bizarrely hyper-sceptical and anti-historical burden of proof to lay on Jesus. The New Testament is a collection precisely of those documents which were regarded as the earliest and most authoritative accounts of the life of Christ and his followers. Naturally, they would have been written down by people who were part of the movement that he launched. Dismissing them because they were written by Christians is a bit like doubting my claim to be married to my wife because those who witnessed us tie the knot were our friends and family, not impartial bystanders. Christian sources inevitably have the theological stamp and reflection of the people who wrote them down, but this doesn't stop them being historical documents, referring to real times, people and places.

Yet even if we were to set aside the Gospels and letters of Paul that testify to Jesus, there are enough extra-biblical, non-Christian sources to put the existence of his life and ministry beyond question. Historians of the time like Tacitus, Josephus and

Pliny the Younger all mention Jesus and the early Church which started gathering to worship in his name. There were also critics of Christianity such as Celsus who, in opposing the early Church, confirmed various aspects of the claims being made about Jesus. The fact that their accounts were written down decades after the events was not at all unusual for the age of antiquity. The histories of most significant figures were written down long after their lives had ended.

When I asked biblical scholar N. T. Wright for the one thing he would show a sceptic as evidence for Jesus' life, he pointed to his death, saying:

> The crucifixion of Jesus of Nazareth is one of the best attested facts in ancient history. The idea that Jesus never existed is something that no ancient historian would take seriously for a minute. If we take Jesus out of the world of first-century Palestinian Judaism, there are a thousand other things that we simply can't explain. All sorts of evidence points back to the certainty of this figure, and particularly his crucifixion.[10]

My plea to those who dismiss the New Testament accounts of Jesus' life as legendary fairy tales is to be consistent with the evidence. In my experience, sceptics often demand a level of proof for Jesus that they never require of any other equivalent historical figure. If the same amount of scepticism they apply to Jesus were applied generally, we would have hardly any history to speak of whatsoever.

But I want to go further than merely saying Jesus was a historical figure who was well attested by those who lived after him. I believe a strong case can be made that the Gospels themselves contain the testimony of first-person eyewitness accounts about his life, death and resurrection. The research has been led primarily by New Testament historian Richard Bauckham, who has appeared on *Unbelievable?* several times to talk about his book *Jesus and the Eyewitnesses.*[11]

While scepticism about the existence of Jesus has been growing among the general public, Bauckham's pioneering work demonstrated how far the academic ground has shifted in the opposite direction. His research explained why the Gospels themselves are filled with telltale signs that the authors were reporting the eyewitness accounts of the very first followers of Jesus.

For instance, Bauckham records how the writings of an early Church father, Papias, show that Mark's Gospel is based primarily on the recollections of Simon Peter. It's evidence that the disciple's first-hand testimony was assumed by the early Christian community, but is also borne out by the fact that Peter plays such a key role in Mark and is included at the beginning and end of the Gospel.

What has perhaps been most remarkable is the way that Bauckham has brought other lines of historical research to bear in his case for the reliability of the New Testament. In 2002, Israeli scholar Tal Ilan published research on how common certain names were among first-century Jews. Analysing the New Testament for the frequency of names and cross-checking it with Ilan's findings showed that there was a striking correlation between the two records. The Gospels are full of the same names that were being used in the time and place that Jesus lived, lending strong support to the conclusion that the Gospels were recorded by people alive at the time, not invented at some hazy distance from the events in a different location.

Bauckham has even challenged the long-held view that John's Gospel is a later theological work produced by an anonymous religious community. Instead, he believes the evidence shows that John was indeed written directly by the 'beloved disciple' of Jesus, and that, despite its more theologically reflective tone, has the greatest claim to be written directly by an eyewitness of Jesus.

These and many other lines of evidence bring us to the conclusion that we have good reasons for treating the stories of Jesus as historically reliable accounts that came from those who knew him. All of which prompts the next obvious question: why should we believe what they said about him?

HOW TO READ THE BIBLE

Before we address that question, I'd like to make an important aside.

While I've argued that the accounts of Jesus and his first followers in the New Testament are historically reliable, we need to make sure we read them intelligently. Both believers and sceptics often make the mistake of approaching the New Testament in the same way they would approach a modern-day newspaper report, ignoring the fact that literary conventions have a tendency to change in the course of 2,000 years.

Many genres of literature are represented within the 66 books that make up the New and Old Testaments. The Gospels conform to a genre we call 'ancient biography', and would have been understood in their time as firmly historical accounts. But that doesn't mean we should expect the same from them that we might expect from modern biographies. Those who wrote ancient biography had a more flexible approach to the way they laid out their material than is usually employed today.

One of the most valuable lessons I've learned over a decade of hosting *Unbelievable?* is seeing the many layers of meaning that the Gospels offer in their pages. Each author has a theological aim as well as a biographical one, and arranges his material accordingly. Matthew is keen to draw out the way Jesus' ministry intersected with the Old Testament, whereas Luke is more interested in how this good news will impact a non-Jewish audience. Mark's Gospel is a rapid-fire account whose urgency seems to reflect its early provenance.

The mistake is to treat the Gospels woodenly as inflexible pieces of reportage. When presented with evidence for their historicity, the sceptic is liable to point out some inconsistency between the accounts as proof that they are unreliable. But purported contradictions often have an explanation in the literary conventions of telescoping and reordering material that the Gospel writers worked within. Many gallons of ink have been spilled in debates over whether the accounts are 'inerrant'. But in my view, to obsess over differences in the details is to focus our energy in the wrong place. We aren't obliged to make every element of the stories line up in order to establish that the Gospels are historically reliable, any more than differing accounts from the battle of Waterloo would change the conclusion that Napoleon's army was defeated.

As a whole, the Bible is a library of books which, given the varied cultures, places and wide timescale they cover, present a remarkably coherent account of God's working in history. I'm a Christian so, while I would affirm that every part of Scripture bears the mark of its human author, I also believe that God has been working in the background to provide a written record for multiple generations about who he is and why he came in the person of Jesus. That's why I use words like 'inspired' and 'authoritative' to describe the Bible. It's more than just an interesting collection of historical records and moral teachings. It stands apart from every other religious and historical record because it reveals the one who is the key to history and salvation itself. Those words exist to make *the* Word of God himself known to us.

I don't expect a sceptic to share that view of course. But if we can merely agree that the Gospels are generally historically reliable, then we already share enough common ground to address the really important question. If Jesus was who he said he was and if he died and rose again, what should our response to him be?

Answering that question takes us beyond simply analysing the evidence for a Jesus who existed a long time ago. It brings us to the question of whether he has a claim on our lives today.

REVERBERATING THROUGH HISTORY

Thousands of Jewish people died by crucifixion under the rule of the brutal Roman Empire in the time of Jesus. It was a uniquely sadistic type of punishment, eventually outlawed as a form of execution because it was deemed too cruel. Yet today, the cross that Jesus died upon has become an extraordinarily potent symbol of love triumphing over hate, peace over pain, and forgiveness instead of fear. It has been represented endlessly in art, fashion and architecture. Through the years it has been banned, burned and blessed. Its mystery continues to divide, reconcile and challenge all kinds of people. To many its message remains the 'foolishness' that Paul spoke of in 1 Corinthians 1.18. But to Christians it is the defining event by which God showed his love for the world.

When I interviewed N. T. Wright about the cross, he said: 'Crucifixion was the most barbaric and horrible way to die in those days. Yet Christians made the cross the symbol of their movement from the very beginning.'[12]

Believing that their crucified Messiah represented God's salvation plan for the world was just about the strangest idea that a group of Jewish followers could have come up with. Nevertheless, the first Christians proclaimed that Jesus died, not as a failed revolutionary, but as a perfect sacrifice through whose death God was reconciling the whole of his disordered creation back to himself. They said that Jesus volunteered himself in our place to suffer all the consequences of the sin, pain and rebellion we have created. They told of how his death was the turning point in a cosmic spiritual battle, in which love battled hate, and love won. Since then generations of Christian believers have claimed to be transformed by trusting in Jesus' death for forgiveness and a new life.

But why should a non-Christian believe it?

I meet plenty of people who are happy to agree that a man called Jesus lived in first-century Judea. They will usually affirm that he was a good moral teacher whose words would have an impact on the world for centuries to come. But believing he was the Son of God whose death paves the way to salvation? That's a step too far. It was C. S. Lewis who most famously captured the inconsistency of such a position:

> I am trying here to prevent anyone saying the really foolish thing that people often say about Him: I'm ready to accept Jesus as a great moral teacher, but I don't accept his claim to be God. That is the one thing we must not say. A man who was merely a man and said the sort of things Jesus said

would not be a great moral teacher. He would either be a lunatic – on the level with the man who says he is a poached egg – or else he would be the Devil of Hell. You must make your choice. Either this man was, and is, the Son of God, or else a madman or something worse. You can shut him up for a fool, you can spit at him and kill him as a demon or you can fall at his feet and call him Lord and God, but let us not come with any patronizing nonsense about his being a great human teacher. He has not left that open to us. He did not intend to.[13]

It has come to be known as the 'liar, lunatic or Lord' trilemma. Critics often respond that adding a fourth category of 'legend' would cause the argument to fail. In this chapter, I have aimed to show that 'legend' is simply not an option on the table. On the contrary, Jesus' blasphemous claims to divinity were precisely what got him crucified. Since then the life and death of Jesus have reverberated through history for the past 2,000 years. The Gospels report real events performed by a real person at a real time.

We have not been let off the hook of C. S. Lewis's challenge. God came in person to show us what he was like and gave up his own life so that we could be reconciled to him. In doing so, Jesus claimed to be Lord, not just of those who followed him then, but of you and me today.

Before I began *Unbelievable?*, I would have assumed that this story, while beautiful, is something we just accept 'by faith'. I've since learned that Christian faith isn't about believing something without evidence, but trusting in someone because of the experience and evidence we've been granted.

Believing that Jesus is Lord isn't pie-in-the-sky-faith-without-evidence. A whole host of factors make sense of my belief that Jesus was who he said he was, and explain why his life and death are at the centre of our story today. In all my years of hosting the radio show, I have heard any number of alternative theories about Jesus Christ. Ironically, it is the orthodox Christian view of Jesus that continues to strike me as the most radical of all: that a first-century Jewish teacher described himself as the Son of God, was crucified for it and rose from the dead in vindication of that claim.

But it is that most extraordinary claim of all – that Jesus rose again – to which we must now turn.

6 Facts that only fit the resurrection

When you have eliminated the impossible, whatever remains, however improbable, must be the truth.

Sherlock Holmes

I rarely get nervous before interviewing guests for my radio show. But as I waited for Derren Brown in the hotel where we were due to meet, my heart was thumping and my palms were sweating. Why? Well . . . because he's Derren Brown, of course.

If you are still none the wiser, it may be that you don't live in the UK where Brown has established himself as a dazzlingly brilliant, and often controversial, illusionist of stage and screen. But it is his unparalleled ability as a 'mentalist' that sets him apart. In the course of his career, he's persuaded normal men and women to rob security vans, push people to their deaths and assassinate TV personality Stephen Fry (or at least to think they were doing so).

As well as pulling off mind-bending illusions and feats of mind control, Brown has also produced a range of TV and stage shows that question belief in the supernatural. Using a mixture of suggestion, 'cold reading', hypnosis and plain old trickery, Brown has the ability to make people believe in God, miracles and the power of prayer faster than you can say 'prestidigitation' (look it up). Yet he is a thoroughgoing atheist himself. His argument is: if I can fool you, then you're probably fooling yourself too.

However, unlike high-profile atheists such as Richard Dawkins, the magician is not primarily known for his non-belief. In my view, his brand of scepticism reaches a far wider audience than the fire-breathing sort that the New Atheists often deal in. Brown isn't preaching to the sceptical choir. His audience is the unfiltered British public who, like me, stand amazed at the stunts he pulls off on TV and stage.

It turns out that Brown is delightful in person, and my initial nerves were soon settled. When I cracked a joke about being worried that he might turn me into an atheist, he batted it away with a roll of his eyes. 'Boring!' he laughs. Apparently, the mind control is reserved for stage and TV.

Brown was a Christian through his teenage years. However, his faith started to wane at university, where he fell in love with the stagecraft of illusion and hypnosis. Seeing the way people could be duped into false beliefs, he began to wonder if the faith he had adopted might be equally self-delusional. He didn't want to believe it on the strength of feelings, he explained: 'I thought the difference was that there has to be an objective, historical, factual event like the resurrection that separates Christianity from just being a subjective circular belief.'

However, when Brown investigated the historicity of Christ's resurrection, he came away convinced that the evidence for it wasn't there. In the end, there was no drawn-out crisis of faith; the illusionist says he shrugged off his former beliefs remarkably quickly.

Our interview broke with the normal format of the *Unbelievable?* show. For once, I hung up my neutral moderator's cap. This was just me and Brown, going back and forth as we debated meaning, purpose, miracles and theology for an hour and a half. Brown was very open to discussing ideas that had once been important to him with someone for whom they still are. I think we both quite enjoyed it.

It reminded me that there's a real danger of Christians (myself included) caricaturing atheists as sneering, cold-hearted haters of religion. I'm sure some of those exist, especially online, but in person, atheists rarely conform to that image. Brown is the kind of person I'd like to share a drink with down at the pub, as are most non-believers I know. In many respects, we live, love and laugh in the same way as each other. We just disagree about the basic nature of reality.

As a Christian, my reality is centred on the person of Jesus Christ. It all begins and ends with him. His death is the defining act of love by a God who came in person to rescue and redeem his broken-yet-beloved creation. And his resurrection is the breaking in of a new world where death, pain and despair will one day be swallowed up in a glorious new creation.

It's a story that has given strength, purpose and hope to millions who have trusted in it. But, of course, the fact that it's a great story doesn't make it true, however comforting it may be. Brown knows the power of telling stories and doesn't begrudge Christians theirs, but says that, in the end, 'it comes down to whether the resurrection was a real event'. At least on that point Derren Brown, the apostle Paul and I myself are all in complete agreement: if Christ has not been raised, our faith is in vain.

A LEAP IN THE DARK?

There's an old gospel hymn, 'I Serve a Risen Saviour', which includes the chorus, 'You ask me how I know he lives – he lives within my heart.' For many years as a Christian, that was my story too. I believed in the resurrection because of a personal experience of 'knowing' Christ. Many others have a similar testimony. When the lights turn on at the moment of conversion, it goes hand in hand with the belief that the Jesus who 'lives within my heart' really did rise from the dead.

But if you had asked me to provide any grounds for that belief in historical terms I would have struggled. There was plenty of evidence that Jesus lived and died, but his resurrection was something we just accepted on 'faith', wasn't it?

It was only in the course of engaging with scholars and sceptics on *Unbelievable?* that I realized a solid historical argument could also be mounted for the resurrection. It equally served as a reminder that Christian 'faith' isn't simply about summoning up the will to believe in something. For many people, a grounded faith involves trusting in Christ on the basis of both personal experience and public evidence. Instead of a leap into the void, this kind of faith is more like taking a step and expecting to land on something solid.

Many sceptics have made that step of faith after investigating the historical circumstances of the resurrection. The American author Lee Strobel wrote his book *The Case for Christ* as an account of how, as a sceptical journalist, he became convinced of Christianity after investigating the evidence. His journey mirrors that of English journalist Frank Morison who, at the start of the twentieth century, began a similar investigative project to prove that the story of Christ's resurrection was a myth. Famously, the book he eventually wrote, called *Who Moved the Stone?*, told the story of how he instead became convinced that Jesus had risen from the dead.

Morison began with a set of assumptions that most people, a hundred years later, continue to hold – that the story of the resurrection, recorded in all four Gospels, is based on superstitious fables that gave rise to a legendary fairy tale. Richard Dawkins has written: 'Accounts of Jesus' resurrection and ascension are about as well-documented as Jack and the Beanstalk.'[1]

When I discussed the resurrection with Derren Brown, I wondered if he might consider it a first-century version of an illusion of the sort he regularly pulls off. But, like Dawkins, he insisted that he doesn't credit the stories to begin with, saying of the Gospels:

> These are sacred stories that are there to show a divine person. It's the equivalent of a cult springing up now around a soldier in World War Two who had died and been resurrected and the evidence they gave you for that was some anonymous, second-hand, written information in the 1980s. How seriously would you be expected to take it?

I pushed back. The analogy wasn't really the same. The Gospels were written down within the lifetime of Christ's followers, as a product of first-hand testimony, not as anonymous second-hand recollections. And why would a group of God-fearing Jews invent such a strange tale, at odds with their typical religious expectations, and which brought so much trouble their way?

We agreed to disagree in the end, but I encouraged the illusionist to revisit the evidence. Brown made up his mind on the resurrection 25 years ago. Had time allowed I would have been interested to hear how he might respond to some of the most recent historical research.

In fact, I believe that the case for the resurrection is stronger today than ever before. A new generation of biblical scholars have been examining afresh the evidence for the claim that lies at the centre of the Christian faith. Leading this field are New Testament historians Gary Habermas and Mike Licona, authors of *The Case for the Resurrection of Jesus*, who have jointly proposed a new way of making the argument – the 'minimal facts' approach.

THE MINIMAL FACTS OF THE RESURRECTION

Christians are often accused by their critics of circular reasoning – believing in the claims of Scripture on the basis of the Bible's own claim to be inspired. True or not, it tends to mean that sceptics assume belief in the divine inspiration of Scripture is a prerequisite to believing its claims about the resurrection of Jesus. But they may be surprised to learn that with the 'minimal facts' approach, no such presupposition is required.

There is no appeal to the inspiration of Scriptures nor even attempts to try to harmonize apparent differences between the Gospel accounts. The aim of the minimal facts approach is far simpler: to show that the resurrection of Jesus is the best explanation for a set of historical facts which *are* agreed upon by the vast majority of New Testament historians, *whether believing or non-believing, Christian or not.*

Habermas has described it as the 'lowest common denominator' version of the facts. These are the ones that are attested by multiple, early sources and pass the criteria of historical reliability. Disputes may arise over various other elements of the Gospel accounts, but for these facts there is a historical consensus that can't be denied.

The claim is that, for those with an open mind, the agreed-upon 'minimal facts' are enough to make the case for the resurrection as the best explanation that unites them all. Different scholars present different lists of facts. Here I'll present five of those that are commonly included and then ask the question: when we combine them together, what is the best explanation for them?

FACT 1: JESUS DIED BY CRUCIFIXION

Jesus' death on the cross is undisputed by historians, as we saw in the previous chapter. Not only is the story found in all four Gospels, but contemporary writers such as the Jewish historian Josephus also record the event.

Interestingly, the main pushback on the historicity of the crucifixion has come not from mythicist atheists, but from Muslims. Although Islam affirms that Jesus was a prophet sent by Allah, the Qur'an claims that he did not die on the cross. Many Muslims believe that a substitute for Christ died in his place. In this regard, the Islamic view of Jesus stands against the vast weight of prevailing scholarship.

When Nabeel Qureshi, a well-known convert from Islam to Christianity, came on *Unbelievable?* to discuss his conversion, he described a turning point in his quest for the truth about Jesus. During his time of searching he came to realize that the Qur'an's position on the crucifixion was historically indefensible. And, if Christ really had died, it opened up the possibility that Christian claims about his resurrection could also be true.

The fact of Jesus' death by crucifixion may be regarded as the most uncontroversial of the five facts. But, as Qureshi's conversion demonstrated, you can't have a resurrection without a dead body to start with. Showing that those who deny the death of Jesus are going against the weight of historical evidence is an important first step.

FACT 2: THE EMPTY TOMB

All four Gospels record that a group of Jesus' female followers discovered his empty tomb on the first day of the week. Not only does this lend the story the historical weight of multiple attestation, but it also affirms this 'minimal' fact in an unexpected way.

I have a confession to make. A few years ago, I was travelling to the offices of our radio station on my normal morning train commute. It was an unremarkable journey, until the point when I reached my required stop. Another passenger was sitting next to me with a laptop resting on the flip-down table in front of him. When I got up to leave my seat, I inadvertently poured my flask of coffee all over his laptop. As you can imagine, he wasn't terribly impressed about it.

The coffee-and-laptop debacle is an event that remains etched in my memory for ever but is one I rarely tell people about. Why? Because I'm embarrassed about it, naturally. And that's generally true in life. Most people are unlikely to tell stories that reflect badly on themselves. But if you do tell an embarrassing story, the chances are it's true.

Historians describe this phenomenon as the 'criterion of embarrassment'. A recorded story is more likely to be true if it would have been embarrassing or inconvenient to those telling it. The sort of stories that we are likely to invent or exaggerate tend to be those that make us look better, not worse.

All four Gospels highlight the discovery of Jesus' empty tomb. And in all four accounts the first people to happen upon the tomb are the women followers of Jesus. Is this something that the Gospel writers would have invented?

In the patriarchal culture of first-century Israel, female testimony was worth far less than that of a man. If the Gospel writers had intended to pull the wool over their readers' eyes, it would have made far more sense to place the male disciples as the first arrivals at the empty tomb, not Mary Magdalene and her companions.

This is where the criterion of embarrassment comes into play. In a first-century context, the discovery of the missing body by women followers would have been 'embarrassing' for early Christians seeking to persuade others, yet it is present in all the accounts. The most plausible reason they included it is because that was how it happened.

Although the fact of the empty tomb is supported by a smaller majority of scholars compared to the other minimal facts,[2] we need to take it seriously. Despite the Gospels differing in their details, the discovery of the empty tomb by a group of Jesus' female followers is central to all four accounts and acts, retrospectively, as a remarkable piece of corroborating evidence for the historical authenticity of the story.

FACT 3: PEOPLE REPORTED MEETING THE RISEN CHRIST

That the followers of Jesus reported experiences of meeting Christ after his death is, again, widely agreed across both believing and non-believing scholarship. The most well-known reports in the Gospels, when Jesus appears to various groups of disciples – on a beach, behind closed doors and on the road to Emmaus – are the stuff of many Easter Sunday sermons. Yet these are not our only historical evidence of Christ appearing to his disciples. The letters of Paul were written even closer to the time of the events and also affirm that the followers of Jesus reported meeting the risen Jesus (as would Paul himself, albeit in a different way).

Could these reported experiences have arisen by a legendary word-of-mouth fashion, in a historical version of 'Chinese whispers' (or the 'telephone game' as my American friends call it)? The historical records don't support that idea. In 1 Corinthians 15, Paul quotes a creed of the Church, affirming the resurrection and the witnesses to it:

> For what I received I passed on to you as of first importance: that Christ died for our sins according to the Scriptures, that he was buried, that he was raised on the third day according to the Scriptures, and that he appeared to Cephas [Peter], and then to the Twelve. After that, he appeared to more than five hundred of the brothers and sisters at the same time, most of whom are still living, though some have fallen asleep. Then he appeared to James, then to all the apostles, and last of all he appeared to me also, as to one abnormally born.
>
> (1 Corinthians 15.3–8)

Paul wrote this letter around AD 55, and was quoting from an already established tradition, which means that these resurrection experiences were being reported from the very inception of the Christian Church. These were not half-remembered reports far removed from the events.

These are the reasons why a non-Christian New Testament scholar like Gerd Lüdemann was able to write: 'It may be taken as historically certain that Peter and the disciples had experiences after Jesus' death in which Jesus appeared to them as the risen Christ.'[3]

Whether historians like Lüdemann believe that these *really were* experiences of the bodily risen Christ is a question we will come to shortly. But that Jesus' followers themselves *believed* that they had seen the risen Jesus is a well-established fact.

FACT 4: THE CONVERSION OF SCEPTICS

Whenever I meet a convert to Christianity, there is invariably an important moment – often a personal experience or the discovery of a vital piece of evidence – that was a turning point in that person's journey. For those who are antagonistic towards Christianity, the strength of the factors that led to conversion must be all the greater to overturn their previous convictions.

From the writings of the New Testament, we know that the apostle Paul (originally known as Saul) and James the brother of Jesus were both sceptics of Christianity in its early years.

As a law-abiding Jew, Paul's persecution of the new Christian sect is well documented in his own letters and the book of Acts. Habermas and Licona write that Paul's subsequent conversion following an appearance of Christ is

> well documented, reported by Paul himself, as well as Luke,
> Clement of Rome, Polycarp, Tertullian, Dionysius of Corinth,
> and Origen. Therefore, we have early, multiple, and firsthand
> testimony that Paul converted from being a staunch opponent
> of Christianity to one of its greatest proponents . . .[4]

In similar fashion, according to the Gospels, James the brother of Jesus was a sceptic of Christ's ministry and movement. But in Paul's letters James is listed as one of the leaders of the Jerusalem church and a witness to the resurrection. James had evidently been converted. In fact, his martyrdom for his belief in Christ is recorded by extra-biblical sources such as Josephus, Hegesippus and Clement of Alexandria.

James and Paul should have been 'hostile witnesses' against the Christian faith, but through their conversion they became key witnesses for the defence. Again, this fact is affirmed by the majority of historians, both Christian and non-Christian. What was the decisive factor in the conversion of those who were otherwise hostile to Christian faith?

FACT 5: THE EXPLOSIVE GROWTH OF THE CHRISTIAN CHURCH

The Monty Python film *The Life of Brian* was not terribly well received by churches when it was released in 1979. But those who criticized it for parodying Christ through its eponymous hero Brian ('He's not the Messiah, he's a very naughty boy!') probably failed to notice that it was correct in at least one respect.

Figures with messianic claims were not uncommon in first-century Judea. Other preachers drew their own followers. The only difference is that when their leaders were killed by the Romans those followers either went home or found themselves a new Messiah. What they did not do was immediately begin to proclaim that their Messiah had risen from the dead.

For starters, it would have been a very un-Jewish thing to say. Jews believed in the general resurrection from the dead at the end of time. There was no expectation of individuals, much less the Messiah, being raised from death before then. Yet this is what Jesus' followers started proclaiming. Again, it would have been a strange thing to make up in order to persuade fellow Jews.

In the process, a group of dejected, defeated and crushed disciples who had lost their leader to a brutal, humiliating death at the hands of the Roman overlords suddenly became a group of bold, extraordinarily confident people willing to be rejected by their Jewish culture, and experience beating, persecution and death for their beliefs.

In the process, the Church grew phenomenally – another well-established fact across the spectrum of New Testament research. In fact, members of this new sect within Judaism were so confident about their claim that Jesus had been raised on the third day, Sunday, that they actually began to meet together to break bread and worship on that day. In the Christianized West, Monday marks the beginning of the working week. But for Jewish people Sunday was the first working day of the week. For the Jesus movement to start meeting for worship on that day while everyone else went about their domestic and commercial lives would have been a huge inconvenience. They must have had a good reason to do so.

What transformative event explains all this? There seems to be a resurrection-shaped hole at the centre of the early Church's growth.

FINDING THE THEORY THAT FITS

These then are some of the historical facts agreed upon by the vast majority of both believing and non-believing New Testament historians. And as in previous chapters, when presented with a set of facts and evidence we must ask the now-familiar question: what is the best explanation?

My simple suggestion is that the explanation that best fits the facts is the one that was given from the beginning. That Jesus really did rise from the dead. Why? Because it is the one which most obviously and easily brings together all the facts.

Naturally, many have sought to put forward alternative theories that don't involve any sort of supernatural conclusions. If we are serious about finding the best explanation, it's important that we consider them. So here are some of the most common contending explanations for the events of Easter and why, when run through the 'minimal facts' filter, each fails to best explain the full set of data.

THE AUTHORITIES STOLE THE BODY

While this explanation gives a rationale for Fact 2, the discovery of the empty tomb, the theory seems to come unstuck when we consider that the Christians caused the authorities a fair amount of trouble as their radical claims turned Jerusalem 'upside down' (Acts 17.6, ESV). It would have been simple enough for the authorities to produce the body, and squash the movement, if they had it in their possession.

Moreover, even if one could posit a plausible reason why the authorities would have wanted to steal the body (and did so without leaving a scrap of historical evidence since no ancient sceptic even claimed this had occurred), one must still explain minimal Facts 3 and 4. How did Jesus' disciples come to genuinely believe he had risen and appeared to them? According to the Gospels, they didn't believe when they saw the empty tomb but believed after seeing him. It also doesn't account for how the sceptics Paul and James came to believe. After all, they would have been the first to suspect someone had taken the body.

The problems posed by Facts 3 and 4 exist for all the rest of the theories too. But let's have a look at them anyway.

THE DISCIPLES STOLE THE BODY

Such an explanation means the disciples would have deliberately fabricated their resurrection stories. As previously mentioned, inventing a story in which a group of women were the first witnesses would have been a bizarre way of perpetrating a resurrection hoax in first-century Jewish culture. Moreover, it made no sense for Jews to do that with a failed Messiah – a resurrection before the end of time went against their theological expectations. The growth of the early Church under persecution is also a factor. Would Christians have experienced trouble and been willing to die brutal deaths for something they knew to be a lie? Perhaps one or two of them. But all of them?

THE FOLLOWERS OF JESUS WENT TO THE WRONG TOMB

Another well-established historical element of the story is that Joseph of Arimathea, someone well known to the early Church, personally made a tomb available which he owned. So why would Jesus' followers have turned up at the wrong place? As well as presuming that the disciples must have been rather unintelligent, this theory doesn't make sense of the experiences of the risen Jesus they reported. Moreover, couldn't the authorities or Jesus' detractors have gone to the correct tomb and verified that Jesus' corpse was still there?

JESUS DIDN'T DIE ON THE CROSS AND WAS LATER RESUSCITATED IN THE TOMB

This explanation tries to account for the empty tomb and resurrection appearances by calling into question the first and best attested fact of all – that Jesus died by crucifixion. Some have suggested that Jesus merely appeared to have died and was later revived in the cool of the tomb. But the Romans were very efficient at killing people by crucifixion and had good reason to be. If they didn't properly execute prisoners, Roman soldiers received severe punishment themselves. The 'apparent death' theory also seems far-fetched as an explanation for the resurrection appearances. After beating, crucifixion and three days in a tomb, the maimed individual who supposedly survived would hardly have been the picture of a supernaturally raised Messiah.

THE WHOLE THING WAS A LEGENDARY FICTION THAT CAUGHT ON

As we've seen, Paul's creedal statement in 1 Corinthians 15 shows that the resurrection was a belief present in the Christian community from the earliest times. There's simply not enough time for an urban legend to have spread so quickly and strongly that it replaced all other accounts of what actually happened. Hopefully the multiplicity of reasons why the disciples had no good reason to invent such a story is also clear. All the minimal facts, especially Fact 5, the explosive growth of the early Church in the face of persecution and the conversion of sceptics, contradict the 'legendary fiction' theory.

THE DISCIPLES EXPERIENCED HALLUCINATIONS OF THE RISEN JESUS

Most sceptical scholars have abandoned the other naturalistic theories in this list. This one still persists today, however. Hallucinations do sometimes occur when people lose loved ones.

The people most likely to experience a grief hallucination are senior adults grieving the loss of a spouse. Approximately 50 per cent do, often believing they hear or sense the person with them. However, only 7 per cent of all senior adults grieving the loss of a loved one experience a visual hallucination of that person. It's also worth noting that people don't experience the same hallucinations – most psychologists agree that mass hallucinations don't occur.[5] In contrast, 100 per cent of the disciples experienced what they believed were visual appearances of Jesus. That's a far greater percentage than can be supported by hallucination research completed during the past century.

Those who propose a 'hallucination theory' also generally assume the disciples must have had a powerful psychological incentive to see Jesus come back to life. However, as we've already seen, the disciples had no pre-existing expectation of a rising Messiah-figure. Jesus' resurrection was unexpected and out of keeping with their Jewish theological expectations. The Gospels repeatedly mention the scepticism of the disciples both to Jesus' foretelling of his death and to the resurrection when it is reported by the women (the men dismiss it as an 'idle tale' in Luke 24.11, ESV). Likewise, Paul had even less reason to hallucinate the risen Christ; he hated the movement Jesus was at the centre of. Resurrection in Jewish terms was also an invariably physical, bodily concept. What the disciples describe in their accounts is a flesh-and-blood, grilled-fish-eating Jesus, and Paul's own resurrection theology is about a real person, not an ephemeral 'spiritual' experience.

We could continue to multiply the number of naturalistic alternative theories, or come up with an implausibly ad hoc hodgepodge of several of them. But when run through the logical filter of the agreed–upon 'minimal facts', none of them manages to unify all the diverse elements of the data we have in front of us. The best explanation for the minimal facts is the one that the first followers gave – that Jesus Christ rose from the dead.

CAN A HISTORIAN BELIEVE IN A MIRACLE?

Unsurprisingly, the resurrection of Jesus is one of the most frequently debated subjects on *Unbelievable?*. It is, after all, the central claim of the faith, and the Christian calendar provides a natural opportunity to revisit the subject every Easter. When Derren Brown and I debated the matter, we did so as lay people. But the debates on *Unbelievable?* frequently feature leading historians on both sides, including Gary Habermas and Mike Licona, who have pioneered the approach outlined in this chapter.

Mike Licona has been involved in numerous debates on my radio show with Bart Ehrman over the years. Both are New Testament scholars whose stories of faith had similar beginnings but diverged dramatically at a later stage. Ehrman let go of his Evangelical Christian faith after encountering perceived problems with the New Testament.

Mike Licona had a similar crisis of faith in the early years of his academic career when his study of the New Testament didn't match what he had been taught about it while growing up. However, whereas Ehrman's study led him away from Christianity, Licona's research convinced him that the resurrection was the only adequate explanation for the historical evidence he found in the Gospels. Other pieces of the puzzle fell into place as Licona began to appreciate how the New Testament accounts reflected the literary conventions of their day rather than the modern standards often imposed on them by both Christians and critics. His recent book, *Why Are There Differences in the Gospels? What We Can Learn from Ancient Biography*, is essential reading in this regard.

During one of his dialogues with Licona on the show, Ehrman rattled off a list of differences between the Gospel accounts of the resurrection, such as the number of women and the accounts of angels at the empty tomb. He argued that these differences give reason to doubt the reliability of the resurrection story. Naturally, Licona knows these differences just as well as Ehrman but he didn't find that they count against the overall strength of the account, saying:

> It is a bit like the *Titanic*. There were conflicting accounts from survivors, such as whether the ship broke in half before sinking or whether it went down in its entirety. But no one called into question whether the *Titanic* sank or not. It was the peripheral details that were in question. It is the same thing with the New Testament. They are all peripheral details that have no impact on the fundamental truth of Christianity.[6]

It's another reminder that the Christian isn't obliged to convince a sceptic of every detail of Scripture to be able to show that belief in the resurrection is a rational position to hold. The average sceptic may also be surprised to learn that Ehrman, despite his scepticism, affirms many of the minimal historical facts proposed by Licona and Habermas, including that the followers of Jesus believed they had experiences of the risen Christ.

Likewise, the agnostic New Testament scholar James Crossley affirms that he broadly agrees with the minimal facts. When he engaged in conversation with Gary Habermas on *Unbelievable?*, he stated that the disciples' belief that they had encountered the risen Jesus was 'the hardest, best evidence we have'.[7]

So what stops scholars like Crossley and Ehrman from believing that what the disciples experienced was *in fact* the resurrected Jesus? Both have given similar explanations for their positions when I've asked them about it – that historians simply cannot posit miraculous explanations for historical events, whatever the evidence may suggest.

Crossley's upbringing in the north of England didn't involve any particularly religious influences, but he became intrigued by biblical studies as a student. His sociopolitical approach has led him to focus on the 'political, social and economic reasons' for the rise of the early Church. As a non-believer he has always provided a model of gracious and open-minded engagement with Christian scholars like Habermas on the show. While he has no interest in knocking people's personal faith commitments, he nevertheless says that he can't infer any supernatural conclusions himself: 'I believe we can only give explanations that go so far. As a historian, I cannot prove [miraculous] claims.'[8]

Ehrman was a little more bullish when interacting with Licona on whether a historian can conclude that a resurrection took place, objecting:

> You've moved from history to faith. You can show historically that people claimed they saw Jesus alive afterwards; you can draw the conclusion that they probably believed it. But if you yourself agree that Jesus was raised from the dead, you are saying that was an act of God in history. What you are doing is no longer history – it's faith.[9]

And there's the rub. For those like Habermas and Licona, no explanation (including those with supernatural implications) should be off limits. But those like Ehrman will always insist that the standard rules of historical enquiry – which excludes miracles by definition – can't be suspended for Christian believers. On this basis, the minimal facts, no matter how well they cohere with the resurrection as an explanation, must be explicable in naturalistic terms. A naturalistic explanation will always supersede a supernatural one. Change those rules and we'd have to let in all sorts of miraculous claims from history, says Ehrman.

FOLLOWING THE EVIDENCE

I understand where historians like Ehrman and Crossley are coming from in refusing to allow a supernatural explanation for a set of historical data. But I also want to ask the question: why should we prefer a naturalistic explanation at all costs?

Most academic disciplines involving science and history abide by the rule of *methodological naturalism*. Simply put, this is the view that we pursue our studies on the assumption that nature operates with law-like regularity and that historical events are normally explicable in natural terms. This principle doesn't conflict with a Christian view of a God who created a world that operates according to natural laws. The problem comes when this approach is conflated with *metaphysical naturalism* – the view that *all that exists* are material things and natural causes. But such an assumption is unwarranted. Fancy-sounding terms aside, to assume that such an atheistic view of reality is required of the historian seems an overreach.

What if, as I aimed to show in the early chapters of this book, the evidence is against a naturalistic worldview and on the side of theism? If there is a God, then why should we cut ourselves off from explanations that involve supernatural agency if that's where the evidence most clearly leads? If we begin with the assumption that there is no God, then no amount of evidence will ever lead to the conclusion that Jesus was raised from death. But if we grant the possibility that there is a God, then the explanation that God raised Jesus from the dead turns out to be the best fit for all the data we have.

And this doesn't mean we must let in all sorts of supernatural claims for all kinds of historical events. In the normal course of things, methodological naturalism is a good rule of thumb. Miracles are, by definition, unusual, and we should remain rightly sceptical of claims that are poorly evidenced. But the resurrection stands unparalleled by other religious claims in terms of its historical evidence. If there were ever a candidate in the sweep of history to whom an event of this kind might happen, it seems entirely appropriate for it to be Jesus. In his life and death, he claimed to be the fulfilment of many of God's messianic promises to Israel in the past, and his unique life and death would go on to have a greater impact on the world than any other character in history.

As you know, I'm writing this book to explain why, after years of hearing the strongest objections to faith from scholars, sceptics and atheists, I still believe in the claims of Christianity. From the outset, I've sought to show that belief in God makes more sense than atheism. In this and the previous chapter, I've also aimed to demonstrate that, if there is a God, then we have good reasons to believe he has revealed himself to us in Jesus Christ. That revelation comes through the words, life and death of Christ recorded for us by his first followers, but most powerfully through the vindication of his divine claims in his resurrection.

So yes, I believe in the resurrection. But not only because of the historical evidence. The fact is, I believed in the resurrection before I was ever introduced to scholars like Habermas and

Licona. On that basis, I believe in the resurrection as much for personal and experiential reasons as anything else. It isn't just a miracle that once took place in a borrowed tomb, but it is a present hopeful reality that makes sense of the world I live in. I believe in the resurrection as the turning point in God's ongoing redemption of the world. I believe in the resurrection because I see it happening in the lives of others who place their faith in Jesus. I believe in the resurrection because it is God's defiant statement that, in a world currently ruled by decay and death, there is a purpose, hope and life that goes beyond the grave.

Yet I also believe God has granted us enough evidence to allow us to make a rational case for the resurrection on historical grounds. For many, this has been an important gateway to faith as they've realized that the biblical accounts are not Dawkins' 'Jack and the Beanstalk' variety, but deserve to be taken seriously as historical claims.

However, that doesn't mean we dispense with faith in favour of clever arguments. Believing in the resurrection means nothing if it remains merely a belief. Faith must still be exercised in the everyday business of trusting in the presence of the resurrected Christ in a world of hurt and pain. Many of the first witnesses to the risen Christ would suffer and die for their convictions. Belief was the easy part – trusting in his hope and promise in the face of persecution is where faith was put into practice. The same is true for those who call themselves Christians today.

7 The atheist's greatest objection: suffering

Suffering has been stronger than all other teaching . . . I have been bent and broken, but − I hope − into a better shape.

Estella, Great Expectations

The arrival of our third child Jeremy did not go as smoothly as our first two. Shortly after birth he was diagnosed with an infection which would require a course of antibiotics. The memory of accompanying the doctor to the intensive care unit and watching him attempt to insert a cannula needle into the tiny wrist of our baby boy is for ever imprinted on my memory.

I was tasked with feeding Jeremy with drops of sugary water as the doctor manipulated his wrist, attempting several times to find a suitable vein that would allow passage for the antibiotics to enter his system and flush out the infection. But no amount of sucrose solution from my plastic syringe could undo the fact that it was a painful business.

How I wished I could explain to my bawling newborn, not yet 24 hours old, that the doctor wasn't being horrid, he was being helpful; that the pain of the needle was necessary; that this wouldn't last for ever; that I loved him.

Since that day (and with Jeremy now a healthy, boisterous six-year-old) I have often thought about the way that experience could be compared to the way we are often unable to recognize the purposes that may accompany suffering in our own lives and in the world that God is in the process of bringing back to himself.

In this chapter, I will attempt to do what many people before me have done – offer an explanation for why, despite the existence of an all-powerful and all-loving God, suffering, pain and evil are allowed to exist in the world. However, whatever justifications I may give, we still need to accept that we are rarely able to see the big picture in the way that God sees it. If there is a God, then even at the heights of human learning, insight and intelligence, we possess only a fraction of the wisdom, knowledge and understanding that informs the eternal perspective he holds. Like my newborn child, we see only the present pain, the sting of the needle. Yet I believe that God is the parent who is both with us in our suffering and also sees the end from the beginning in ways that we cannot fathom.

I always feel like a bit of a fraud when speaking from my own limited experience about suffering. Up to the present I've led a relatively peaceful life, unmarked by any great tragedy. Expressing opinions about suffering is bound to sound shallow when I've had little of my own to worry about. Nevertheless, I have had the opportunity to speak with and interview many other people who have endured remarkable adversity.

My grandfather Geoffrey Mowat was one of the most memorable. He spent his early career in the colonial service in Malaysia, and became a prisoner under the Japanese during the Second World War. A newly married man, he was separated from his wife Louise for the entirety of the war, and among other trials experienced the misery of 'Hellfire Pass' where the forced labour of emaciated prisoners of war was used to construct the Burma railway. In total, some 60,000 Allied POWs worked on the project. Whether from brutalization, exhaustion or sickness, more than 12,000 died during the railway's construction.

I was able to record a radio documentary with Geoff about his experiences a few years before he passed away. He shared the poignant memory of working in a makeshift hospital tent, where he was charged with the care of 21 young Welsh conscripts suffering from jungle diseases and malnutrition. None of them survived. My grandfather did, however, and his response as a Christian to the suffering he witnessed has stayed with me ever since. I shall trace more of his story later in this chapter.

There have also been many conversations with atheists and non-believers on suffering and evil on *Unbelievable?* over the years. Unsurprisingly, any debate on the existence of God, if left to run long enough, will eventually turn to the question: 'Well, if your God really does exist, how can he allow all the suffering in the world?' It's been asked by people like Alom Shaha, a physics teacher and author of *The Young Atheist's Handbook*.

Shaha was born as a Muslim in Bangladesh but grew up in London. In conversation on the programme, he shared how his mother passed away when he was 13, an event which deeply affected the teenager and was part of the journey that led him to reject Islam and embrace atheism. This was a brave decision in a culture where openly rejecting your religious upbringing can bring shame and exclusion. He explained why he could not reconcile his childhood religion with his growing scientific education, nor find satisfactory evidence for the God his parents believed in. But Shaha's rejection of God struck me as more than just intellectual, with the loss of his mother providing the final confirmation. 'My mother's death made me feel very keenly the absence of God in my life,' said Shaha. 'It wasn't a case of me being angry at God. It was just the finality of her death and the injustice of her life that made me think there wasn't a God.'

Shaha was another guest who disproved the stereotype of the cold-hearted, rationalistic atheist. He spoke movingly of his mother, saying:

> She loved us unconditionally in a way that I perhaps feel God ought to. When she was alive and well, I don't think there was a time when I didn't feel safe in the world, special and loved. Once she was gone, there didn't seem to be any rhyme or reason to that.[1]

Many other atheists have shared similar reasons with me for doubting the existence of God in a world marked by pain and evil. Apart from personal experiences of loss like Shaha's, the case is often made against God on the basis of global suffering. War, famine, disease and natural disasters are all brought up as evidence against God. If God has created this world, why is it so prone to pain, suffering and injustice, and why does he not intervene if he has the power to do so?

IS THERE A RHYME OR REASON?

The problem of suffering is unquestionably the single most important objection to God that has ever existed and ever will. But, before we begin to look at some possible responses, it's worth pointing out a few facts that help frame the issue to begin with.

First, if you were actually to tally up the number of arguments in favour of theism and in favour of atheism, you might be surprised to see an imbalance between the two. On the side of theism there is a multiplicity of arguments – cosmological, philosophical, evidential, moral, ontological, and the list goes on. I presented just a few of them in the early chapters of this book. Atheism, however, while frequently critiquing the role of religion and its arguments for God, has an overall much shorter list of arguments of its own in favour of a naturalistic worldview, the prime one being the argument from suffering.

In this respect, I've often felt that the weight of arguments in favour of theism is frequently underappreciated by sceptics. They may dispute their validity, but the preponderance of arguments tips the scales towards belief in God. While the problem of suffering is a serious objection (enough to warrant book-length responses), as a single argument against God it must nevertheless do a great deal of work on the atheistic side of the scales to counter the weight of the arguments that affirm theism on the other. Pointing out the existence of pain does not necessarily negate the other aspects of our existence and experience that seem to affirm the reality of God.

Second, I have doubts about whether the sceptical question being posed about suffering even makes sense. As I argued in Chapter 3, it's difficult to see how the reality of a world of moral right and wrong can exist in the absence of God. But the question being asked by the atheist is a fundamentally moral one. Suffering often takes the form of injustice and evil perpetrated by humans, and the goodness of God himself is called into question when he is accused by the atheist of being unjust for allowing such pain to exist. Yet without a transcendent source from which they stem, these moral claims about right and wrong, goodness and injustice, are simply our own illusions mapped on to an indifferent physical world. The question only makes sense if there is a God who grounds our moral beliefs to begin with.

We have already noted how C. S. Lewis was moved away from atheism when he wrote:

> My argument against God was that the universe seemed so cruel and unjust. But how had I got this idea of just and unjust? A man does not call a line crooked unless he has some idea of a straight line. What was I comparing this universe with when I called it unjust?

Lewis went on to say:

> Of course I could have given up my idea of justice by say-ing it was nothing but a private idea of my own. But if I did that, then my argument against God collapsed too – for the argument depended on saying that the world was really unjust, not simply that it did not happen to please my private fancies. Thus in the very act of trying to prove that God did not exist – in other words, that the whole of reality was senseless – I found I was forced to assume that one part of reality – namely my idea of justice – was full of sense.[2]

A final fact to bear in mind is that getting rid of God does not get rid of the problem of suffering, evil and injustice. On a Christian worldview, why God allows so much suffering is a massive and painful question, but one that we hope one day to understand. It is a mystery we believe will be answered in a day of final justice and joy when Jesus Christ sets the world to rights. On the atheist worldview there is no such hope for a resolution to the question. There is no question. Suffering is simply a brute fact of existence. There is no 'rhyme or reason' (to borrow Shaha's phrase) in a world without God. Eliminating God may help us to resolve a theological conundrum, but it does not get us any further in terms of the existential question. What meaning can we derive from a world governed by chance in which injustice, pain and death inevitably prevail in so many lives? Within Christian belief, suffering is at least a mystery we can hope to make sense of. In atheism, it is simply meaningless.

So the problem of evil and suffering cuts both ways – it has ramifications for the atheist as well as the Christian. But the objection still remains for believers. How are we to explain the pain we experience if the God that we believe in is so loving and powerful?

What follows are technically termed 'theodicies', rational justifications for why God may have reasons to allow pain and suffering in ways that are compatible with his love and power. But there is always a danger with presenting an apologetic on pain. A clinical approach to an emotional problem can seem terribly cold and unfeeling. I remember well the response to an edition of *Unbelievable?* when the agnostic sceptic Bart Ehrman (yes, he's been on a lot) presented his case against God. He was in conversation with Richard Swinburne, one of the world's leading Christian philosophers. Ehrman elucidated the problem of evil with his usual eloquence, telling stories of seemingly gratuitous suffering. Swinburne in turn responded with an unfaltering philosophical rebuttal. But the response of the listeners was divided. Some, whose minds work with the same logical precision as Swinburne's, hailed him the victor. Others, both Christian and atheist, judged that his responses lacked the empathy needed in the face of such emotional accounts of suffering.

As an apologist, I may be able to reel off a list of reasons why the existence of suffering does not logically disprove God.

But my wife, as a church minister, does a job that is a thousand times harder and arguably much more important. She is at the coalface of people's lives – sitting alongside them as they deal with tragedy, pain and grief. In those situations, people who are actually going through suffering need our love, not our logic. They need someone to sit and weep with them, not to present a three-point sermon on why God allows evil. It is only once we have done the work of comforting people in their anguish that we should attempt to offer reasons (if they ask for them). And even then, we can only offer general principles. We are rarely in a position to know why God allows specific instances of suffering. So with those caveats in place, here are several reasons I would offer for why God allows suffering.

BECAUSE GOD WON'T ROB US OF FREE WILL

Perhaps the most common response to the problem of suffering is known as the 'free will defence'. After all, where does most of the evil in this world come from? Much of it is a direct conse-quence of our wrong choices as human beings. Yet one of the greatest goods that God has given us is free will – the ability to choose between right and wrong. The problem is that many people choose to do evil rather than good.

Imagine if God intervened at every moment anyone was going to make a wrong choice. Freedom of action would no longer exist. If God waved his magic wand to undo every instance where we made a bad choice, we would merely be puppets con-trolled by a puppeteer who overruled our thoughts and actions. Would we want to live in such a world, even if it meant we were insulated from suffering? Could we even speak of concepts such as goodness, generosity and love without them being freely given, and freely rejected?

The Hitlers, Maos and Stalins of this world have wreaked terrible evils on the world. Why does God does not step in supernaturally to put an end to such monstrous dictators? One answer is that to do so would force a greater evil on the world – the banishing of a world in which humans make free decisions. Instead, God gifts us with the awesome responsibility of creating the kind of world we want to live in. In the freedom we have been granted, we are each called upon to stand for good against evil, right against wrong. When my grandfather received beatings at the hands of his captors, or saw his colleagues die from malnutrition and jungle sickness, he didn't blame God. He saw the choices humans freely make for good and evil, and chose to use the limited freedom he had in his prison camp to make what difference he could for good.

So the great gift of freedom and love that God has given us comes at the cost of the evil that people freely choose to carry out in the world.

The critic of Christianity will be quick to reply, 'That may be. But there is also much suffering that exists in the world which isn't a result of our own actions.' Think of natural disasters, disease and illness. Often these are termed 'natural evil' and are presented as a serious challenge to the concept of a loving God. However, even in these cases we shouldn't be too hasty to discount the consequences of the misuse of our human freedom.

The Haiti earthquake which caused so much death and suffering in 2010 was no more violent than the ones which often strike places such as Los Angeles with little or no loss of life. The difference is that compared to Haiti, the USA is a rich and prosperous country with the necessary resources for earthquake-proofed buildings, emergency services and infrastructure.

The fact is that collective human choices have resulted in a world of haves and have-nots – where the impact of natural disasters and disease will very much depend on where you are born in the world. Our free will still makes a huge difference to the toll of natural evil. We can't always lay the blame at God's door.

BECAUSE WE LIVE IN A SPIRITUAL WAR ZONE

But why has God allowed death, disease and natural disaster to exist at all? This question can only be answered by a Christian from within his or her own worldview, and means we must expand our perspective to a cosmic scale.

The apostle Paul states that 'We know that the whole creation has been groaning as in the pains of childbirth right up to the present time' (Romans 8.22). The Christian story is that the whole created order is in some sense 'out of kilter' at a cosmic level. Some theologians trace this to human rebellion – an outworking of 'the fall' which acts both forwards and backwards in time. Others point to the existence of an earlier rebellion in the angelic realm that sparked a 'cosmic fall' (hinted at in Revelation 12.9).

Whatever the origin, the result is a world that is not as it should be. Yet Paul includes the promise that one day 'the creation itself will be liberated from its bondage to decay and brought into the freedom and glory of the children of God' (Romans 8.21).

There has historically been a danger among apologists of preferring to defend a 'God of the philosophers' rather than the God presented to us in Scripture. We may be happy to debate abstractly the philosophical qualities of the former, but be slightly embarrassed at the passionate, untamed, supernatural Yahweh of the Bible. Indeed, the average atheist may scoff at the idea of an angelic and demonic realm that has an influence upon the physical world we inhabit. However, throughout the New Testament we are presented with a worldview of spiritual warfare in which God has chosen his people to be fellow combatants waging a war, not against flesh and blood, but against spiritual 'principalities [and] powers' (Ephesians 6.12, RSV) through our prayer, love and action.

I have increasingly seen that this 'warfare' view of reality may help those who have experienced great suffering to understand that God is not the author of their pain. One such person is Jessica Kelley, whom I interviewed about the loss of her four-year-old son Henry to brain cancer as related in her book *Lord Willing?*. Radio hosts are supposed to 'keep it together' on air, but I failed to hold back my own tears as she told me the story of her little boy's painful struggle and death, despite the prayers of their church community and the best efforts of doctors. Yet Jessica says that her crisis wasn't compounded by a crisis of faith.

Jessica had come to reject what she terms the 'blueprint' view of a God who creates pain and suffering as part of his sovereign plan. Instead she embraced the warfare view, that we live in a world where natural disasters, disease and evil are tied up not only with the choices of human beings but with the freedom exercised by spiritual forces in rebellion against God. Although the war was decisively turned towards victory through the death and resurrection of Jesus, there still remains a world of running spiritual battles. We pray 'Thy will be done on earth as in heaven' precisely because God does not always get his will on earth. Jessica found it helpful to know that the death of her four-year-old to brain cancer was not God's will. Henry was a casualty in the ongoing battle to redeem a fallen and broken world:

> It was incredibly freeing to know when we saw beautiful things happen, when people were coming to the house with casseroles and gifts – we could say, 'This is from God. God is doing everything possible to maximise good.' And when we saw our son suffer and the pain and death, I could say 'this is not from God'. That meant I could maintain a passionate faith in the midst of such terrible loss.[3]

Nevertheless, Jessica's view is controversial to some. Many would object that a God who isn't in control of the whole show isn't the God of the Bible. Calvinist theologians believe that God is the author of both joy and sorrow and, even though we may struggle to see it, works through both for his ultimate purposes and glory. They say the warfare view contains too much of the same sort of randomness in suffering that the atheist must contend with. Jessica finds Calvinism an unhelpful theology, but others have found solace in such a view of God's meticulous sovereignty. As is often the case in Christianity, one size doesn't fit all, and different believers will prefer different theodicies to make sense of God's role in suffering.

Ultimately, whether we take the Calvinist or warfare view, every Christian has experienced living in the tension of a broken world. The groaning of creation brings both good and bad across our path. The natural laws that operate are both a blessing and a curse. Tectonic plate activity renews the surface of the earth with minerals, yet wreaks havoc when humans build cities on the fault lines. Cell replication allows our bodies to grow and develop, yet can result in cancer when natural processes misfire. Death is a necessary part of the cycle of life, yet still remains our 'last enemy' (1 Corinthians 15.26).

The Christian story is of a broken and rebellious creation that is awaiting the renewal of all things. In this view of suffering, Christians are called to live faithfully for the kingdom that has already come in Jesus, while awaiting the kingdom yet to be in which '"He will wipe every tear from their eyes. There will be no more death" or mourning or crying or pain, for the old order of things has passed away' (Revelation 21.4).

BECAUSE SUFFERING CAN DRAW PEOPLE TO GOD

You may have noticed that so far I've used the phrase 'God allows' suffering to impinge upon our lives, rather than 'God causes' suffering. I have never quite been able to reconcile myself to the idea that God actively wills the suffering and evil that people experience. Nevertheless, I still hold the view that God may yet work through the circumstances of our suffering to bring about a set of greater purposes in our lives than may have otherwise been possible. I don't claim to know how God is able to achieve that, but I believe, in his wisdom and power and free of the constraints of time and space that we inhabit, he can. Indeed, there may be aspects of suffering and disaster in which we may never perceive any ultimate good or purpose for the people affected. That is where the active part of faith comes into play – trusting the goodness of the God that we do know for the things that we do not. Nevertheless, there are various ways that we can observe how suffering, as awful as it is, may be used by God in some instances for certain kinds of good.

Underlying many people's questions about suffering is an unquestioned assumption about why God created us in the first place. But what if we stopped to examine that assumption and first ask the question 'What does a loving God *want* for the human beings he created?'

Here are two possible answers: 'It's God's job to keep human beings happy, comfortable and pain-free.' That's what a lot of people assume is meant by God being 'loving'. But there is another possible answer: 'God's purpose for human beings is to bring them to know and love him.' Those are two very different responses. Coming to know and love God may be quite different from being kept comfortable and happy.

The reality is that comfort tends to make us forget about God. It's evidenced by a prosperous Western world where belief in God is increasingly absent. Yet Christianity often thrives in places which are experiencing the fires of persecution or hardship. For some, suffering leads to an abandonment of belief in God, but for many the opposite is true – it causes them to seek God in a world that seems absurd without him.

Another memorable interview I had for *Unbelievable?* was with Will Pearson-Gee who, as a young father, experienced the tragedy of losing both his wife and one of his children in a terrible road accident. His wife had been returning from a day at the beach with their two children when her car, for reasons unknown, swerved into the path of an articulated lorry. Will's world fell apart, but when called upon to identify their bodies in the mortuary he recalls a defining moment:

> They pulled back the white sheets and I ranted, and I screamed, and I wept. Then I looked at them, and I thought

'This cannot be the end.' There was so much life, particularly in my little boy – he was such a handful. I just couldn't believe it was the end of him. At the time I was definitely a 'nominal' Christian. I believed there was some higher power, but I really had no idea about his character or whether he cared about me. Then my eye was drawn to a very simple crucifix on the wall of the mortuary. It was a sign of the Christian faith to which I had been exposed since I was a child but never really thought anything about. It's like a penny dropped, and it suddenly became not just a cross, but a sign of hope for me. I then realized that, if there was all this talk about resurrection and life after death, I needed to find out more about it.[4]

Will went on to become a Christian and eventually followed a calling to ministry as an Anglican priest. He says that, while he would never have wished the accident to happen, he has nevertheless seen the biblical imperative 'that in all things God works for the good of those who love him' (Romans 8.28) proved true in his own life.

C. S. Lewis wrote in *The Problem of Pain*: 'God whispers to us in our pleasures, speaks in our conscience, but shouts in our pain: it is His megaphone to rouse a deaf world.'[5] Like Will, many people have counted pain and suffering as crucial parts of their journey towards Christianity. I know of many others who would describe themselves as having been in a place where they were quite self-sufficient, comfortable and happy in themselves. As Lewis might put it, they were deaf to God. But when circumstances came which stripped them of their security and comfort, their only option left was to turn to God and, in the process, find the thing they had truly been searching for all along.

Such a way of thinking about suffering also applies to the way our own lives and character can ultimately be shaped, if we are willing, to more resemble the character of God.

It can be argued that meaningful moral and spiritual growth as human beings requires a world where some suffering and need exists. I cannot be generous unless there is someone who has less than me. I cannot show compassion unless there is someone who needs caring for. Equally, there are things I may only be able to learn and value when I am placed in a situation of vulnerability and need. We have close friends whose second child was born with Down's syndrome, a condition which has led to them having to significantly reorder their lives around their daughter's disability. It is a life they neither expected nor asked for. Yet they would not swap the life they have. Their daughter is a source of joy who has taught them more about themselves and the things that matter in life than they could have hoped to know otherwise.

Equally, perhaps we can think of a painful situation we've gone through and, even though we wouldn't wish it upon anyone, looking back we can see that we became a better, more truly human person because of it. We probably also know people who have gone through traumatic life experiences, and have consequently been able to help others in similar circumstances. Those who run Alcoholics Anonymous groups are usually those who have passed through the fire of addiction themselves. Those who run bereavement counselling are frequently those who have experienced great loss.

I believe that God is masterful enough to be able to weave many of the experiences and tribulations of our lives into a tapestry that is ultimately beautiful to behold. Yet, in the present, we often only see the tangled mess of threads on the underside of the tapestry. The big picture is something we can usually only recognize in hindsight, as we see how painful experiences have shaped us. At the same time, I want to avoid the danger of simply palming off the reality of suffering with trite clichés. Simplistic apologetic explanations can do more harm than good in insensitive hands. There are many griefs and sorrows we would all swap in a heartbeat if we could. Some things are just plain awful and can't be dressed up any other way. There are many questions we will never see answered this side of eternity. Sometimes we will come to an end of trying to explain things and can only throw ourselves on the mercy of God.

BECAUSE THE GOD OF THE CROSS SUFFERED WITH US

The Bible is not afraid to talk about the raw ugliness of suffering. The book of Psalms is the Bible's hymn book but, unlike our modern disposition to sing uplifting choruses in church, contains as many songs of desolation and lament as it does songs of praise and worship. None perhaps more so than Psalm 22, which begins: 'My God, my God, why have you forsaken me? Why are you so far from saving me, so far from my cries of anguish?'

Questioning, berating and being angry with God may be a natural part of the process of coming to terms with pain. As already noted, none of the 'theodicies' I've outlined so far is likely to help anyone at the point of his or her need. In the course of writing this chapter, I happened to read an anguished Facebook entry from a professor of apologetics who is going through a very difficult family situation. More than anyone, he would know every intellectual response on offer. But in his online post he was simply an exasperated human being asking 'God, when will this let up?'

Sometimes people need to weep, scream and lament. We are told that even Jesus wept when presented with the death of his friend Lazarus. People who are in the where-are-you-God Psalm 22 moment – the loss of a child, the fracturing of a relationship, the delivery of terrible news – don't need a rationale. What people need in such a time is someone to sit with them, weep with them, pray with them, love them. And if there is a time for words, it is to let them know that God himself understands how they feel, for he himself has chosen to enter into our suffering: God himself suffers when we suffer.

This is the shocking truth about the God that Christians worship. He chose to get involved. When he came to earth in the person of Jesus, he shared our joys and he shared our sorrows too. He suffered rejection, betrayal, beating, humiliation and death.

That's why it is so significant that we find the words of Psalm 22 on the lips of Jesus as he hangs on the cross. The psalm, written hundreds of years before the invention of Roman cruci-fixion, prophetically describes Christ's isolation, humiliation and even the manner of his death:

> A pack of villains encircles me;
> they pierce my hands and my feet.
> All my bones are on display;
> people stare and gloat over me.
> They divide my clothes among them
> and cast lots for my garment.
>
> (Psalm 22.16–18)

And when Jesus cries out, 'My God, my God, why have you forsaken me?', we are meant to understand that Jesus himself suffers the worst fate of all – alienation from God as he bore the weight of our sin.

This is the paradox of the Incarnation. Deity itself is on the cross. God comes in person and he suffers for us and with us. We often hear about Emmanuel, 'God with us', at Christmas, but the cross of Easter is where we see it in the most radical way. The cross means many things, but one of them is that God knows what we go through in pain, suffering, humiliation and fear, because he's been through them too. That's at the heart of the Christian story. Life is messy, ugly, and hurts at times, but we have a God who comes alongside and says, 'I know what it feels like.' That alone, while it doesn't take away the hurt, can be enough to enable someone to hang on.

Equally paradoxically, the Christian faith, far from causing people to resign themselves to a broken world, has been the prime motivation for millions to go out and change it. Wherever you find the worst deprivation, poverty and sadness, you will consistently find Christians building hospitals, offering food programmes, bringing education and working for human dignity, often at great expense to their own comfort. In the words of Jesus, quoting Isaiah 61, Christians are people who claim to be filled with Christ's own Spirit in order 'to proclaim good news to the poor . . . to proclaim freedom for the prisoners and recovery of sight for the blind, to set the oppressed free' (Luke 4.18). Which is why, when people ask 'Where is God when tragedy strikes?', the Christian can answer honestly, 'He's right there, in the midst of it.'

Being a Christian offers no magical exemption from the trials of life. In fact, being a Christian may bring with it more suffering than we'd otherwise experience, as those who live under threat of persecution and death for their faith know only too well. The fact that God suffered with us on the cross is not a theodicy in the typical sense. It does not seek to explain away suffering, but it does give countless people the resources to bear it, and perhaps eventually to find a purpose through the pain.

This was ultimately the experience of my grandfather when he cared for the sick and dying men of Tent 13. While Geoff was able to offer some comfort to the men, and was assisted by the padre in their final hours, he felt ill-equipped to deal with their spiritual needs. 'It was these experiences which led me to question the purpose of my life . . . and to wonder if the God who had preserved me so far had something more for me,'[6] he recalled. It led to a major redirection of his post-war career into ministry in the Church of England. There were many more challenges to overcome. These included resuming his relationship with my grandmother Louise (they had spent longer forcibly separated than together as a married couple), and finding the strength to forgive the Japanese, something he says only the example of Christ was able to bring about in his own life.

I BELIEVE IN OSCAR WILDE'S GOD

The problem of suffering is the oldest one of all. From the book of Job, written thousands of years ago, to the present day, people continue to ask the 'Why?' question. One of the most recent and well-publicized examples was provided by the atheist TV presenter Stephen Fry.

When an online video interview of Fry angrily denouncing God as an 'evil, capricious, monstrous maniac', who sits idly by while children die from bone cancer, went viral in 2015 (and continues to pop up, even now, in my Facebook feed), it was proof that the subject of religion still stirs strong emotion, even in a largely secular society. What he said was not particularly new, but the combination of Fry's celebrity, eloquent delivery and visceral emotion caught the attention of many.

On this occasion, rather than record a radio debate on what he had said, I chose to record my own video response titled 'Dear Stephen . . . I Believe in Oscar Wilde's God'.[7] And rather than attempt to give the sort of arguments I've attempted to convey in this chapter, I chose simply to tell a children's story written by his literary hero, Oscar Wilde. It's one I've read to my own children many times.

Wilde's story *The Selfish Giant* tells of a garden where children used to play, but because of the selfishness of the giant who lives there, it is always winter and never spring. After spending years in bitter solitude, the giant one day sees a child trying to climb a tree. His heart thaws and he lifts the child into the branches, prompting the tree to burst into bloom. Spring returns, the children come back out to play, but the giant doesn't see the child again until he is an old man.

One day he sees the child beneath the tree once more and rushes to him. But the giant's joy turns to anger when he sees nail prints in the child's hands and feet. 'Who hath dared to wound thee?' he demands. The child replies: 'Nay, but these are the wounds of love.' Wilde writes:

> 'Who art thou?' said the Giant, and a strange awe fell on him, and he knelt before the little child.
>
> And the child smiled on the giant and said to him, 'You let me play once in your garden; today you shall come with me to my garden, which is paradise.'
>
> And when the children ran in that afternoon, they found the Giant lying dead under the tree, all covered with white blossoms.[8]

It's a simple story, but one that also beautifully captures the heart of the Christian story. Wilde recognized that God is not a tyrant who makes the world an evil place. In a world that has been bent out of shape because of us, where winter reigns and the blossoms are few and far between, we have a God who has entered the darkness and borne it himself. The wounds of love define this God who entered our winter world as a child and later, on a tree, with nail-scarred hands and feet, ushered in the dawn of the spring and our own hearts' redemption so that we too may join him in his garden one day.

That's not an argument that answers the atheist's objections, but Wilde tells a very different story about God from the one told by Stephen Fry. I've no idea whether he has seen my video response, but I hope at least some of those who have watched his video will have watched mine too, because we are describing God from two very different perspectives.

One is informed by the assumption that God, if he exists, owes us a quiet, comfortable life in a world free from pain. God is the divine childminder whom we should dismiss when he doesn't live up to our expectations. The other view is of a Father God who passionately pursues us through the pleasure and pain that exists both within us and in the world around us. I even dare to believe that a world in which Christ stepped in – freely giving his life on the cross for his broken creation in order to demonstrate the supreme love of the Father – may be the best possible kind of world we could hope for. For in that world, pain and suffering are not unremitting brute facts of existence, but things that the God of both the cross and the resurrection can turn into his greatest victory.

8 My ten minutes with Richard Dawkins

To you, I'm an atheist. To God, I'm the loyal opposition.
Woody Allen

It was 21 October 2008, and I was in a long line of people waiting for the heavy oak doors of Oxford's Natural History Museum to swing open. We were queuing for a long-awaited debate between Richard Dawkins and John Lennox, due to take place inside. It was the second in a series of encounters between the two professors, sponsored by the US-based organization The Fixed Point Foundation. The first debate had been in Birmingham, Alabama. For the UK event, Oxford University's Museum of Natural History had been chosen in tribute to another famous debate that once took place there. In 1860, following the publication of Darwin's *On the Origin of Species*, Bishop Samuel Wilberforce, a noted clergyman, and Thomas Huxley an atheist champion of Darwin's work on evolution, had crossed swords on whether God or nature alone explained human life. Little had changed in 150 years.

Tonight's debate had attracted national attention and the place was full. As the audience took their places, the Gothic arches that rose above us were in the same style as the many churches that dotted Oxford. But this sanctuary was dedicated to the pursuit of understanding through science. The massive dinosaur skeletons which towered among the arches provided a suitably dramatic backdrop to the two debaters who had taken the stage.

Both were professors of science at the university. John Lennox's disciplines were mathematics and the philosophy of science, but he had also established a reputation as an engaging and erudite Christian speaker and debater. Richard Dawkins needed little introduction. Having made his name as a biologist, he had subsequently held a specially created position of Professor of Public Understanding of Science. Anyone who had heard the atheist on the subject of science and religion was in no doubt about his understanding of the question under debate: has science buried God?

I was glad to see that the debate was conversational in format (I wondered if someone had taken a leaf from the book of *Unbelievable?*). The dialogue ran across familiar territory – the biblical and evolutionary accounts of origins, the debate over whether cosmology pointed to God, arguments from reason, morality and even the person of Jesus himself. Lennox was able to get Dawkins to admit he had made a mistake in *The God Delusion* by citing a professor of German who believed Jesus was a myth, when nobody in the relevant field of historical studies took that view. Nevertheless, Dawkins dismissed the story of Jesus as 'provincial'. If there were a God who governed the universe, what a strange way to act in history . . . through an itinerant preacher in a small backwater of the Roman Empire 2,000 years ago.

I enjoyed the interaction and, planning to review it for the radio show, was hoping to be able to interview both the participants afterwards. Lennox had previously contributed to the programme as a guest, but I had yet to snare the biggest catch – a recording with Dawkins himself. I had never met him, much less interviewed him. The good news was that I had been invited to a post-event party at a nearby college and I had brought my handheld recorder in the hope of being able to catch Dawkins in person if he showed up.

Once the press conference and book signings were over, I left the museum and began to walk down the street to where the gathering was taking place. To my great surprise I found myself walking alongside none other than Dawkins himself, pushing a bicycle at his side (the chief form of transport for many Oxford residents). I didn't feel I could whip out my microphone there and then, but I introduced myself and we had some conversation as we made our way to the college. He was polite, but looked somewhat dubious when I told him my profession. A *Christian* radio station, you say? I imagine you qualify as a charity like so many churches? He grumbled about the difficulty that his own non-profit organization, the Richard Dawkins Foundation for Reason and Science, had experienced attaining charitable status. The encounter was a brief one, but I told him I hoped to catch him for an interview once inside.

As the canapés and wine were distributed I circulated around the room, which was abuzz with conversation. I interviewed several students about what they had made of the debate, I spoke to Larry Taunton, director of the Fixed Point Foundation, and also to Lennox, who admitted he'd been daunted by the occasion but thought it had gone reasonably well. All that was left was to interview Dawkins himself. He was constantly surrounded by people, so I had to choose my moment. He had just finished with Melanie Phillips, a sharp-tongued right-wing newspaper columnist. He looked a bit cross. It turned out that Phillips' subsequent article made much of his admission during the debate that 'a serious argument could be made for a deistic God'. Dawkins ripped into Phillips on his own website soon after the piece appeared.

My heart was in my mouth as I stepped up to the professor and reintroduced myself, microphone in hand. 'Don't fluff this, Justin' was all I was thinking. Whether he was in the mood or not for another debate, I plunged straight in, cross-examining him on some of the issues that had been raised. Wasn't his view of a purposeless universe a bit bleak? Can concepts like love be reduced to chemical processes? He responded that the universe doesn't owe us a purpose. As to love, he was as romantic as the next man, but introducing God wouldn't make him appreciate love, romance or poetry any more. We also talked about cosmology, and morality too.

This is perhaps where the most interesting part of our discussion happened. I'm not one for big 'gotcha' moments. The natural flow of a conversation doesn't always give much scope for nuance when thinking on your feet. Still, when I pressed the professor on whether we can really believe that morality is derived only from godless, undirected evolution alone, his answer was revealing. Here's how our interaction went:

> ME (JB) But if we'd evolved into a society where rape was considered fine, would that mean that rape *is* fine?

> DAWKINS (RD) I don't want to answer that question. It's enough for me to say that we live in a society where it's not considered fine. We live in a society where selfishness, failure to pay your debts, failure to reciprocate favours is regarded askance. That is the society in which we live. I'm very glad — that's a value judgement — glad that I live in such a society.

JB But when you make a value judgement don't you yourself immediately step outside this evolutionary process and say that the reason this is good . . . is that it's good? And you don't have any way to stand on that statement.

RD My value judgement itself could come from my evolutionary past.

JB So therefore it's just as random, in a sense, as any product of evolution.

RD You could say that. In any case, nothing about it makes it more probable that there is anything supernatural.

JB OK. But ultimately, your belief that rape is wrong is as arbitrary as the fact that we've evolved five fingers rather than six.

RD You could say that, yeah.[1]

After it aired on *Unbelievable?*, this part of the conversation was picked up by a number of other commentators. In doing some background reading before beginning this book, I even discovered that the exchange is quoted in the book *Mere Apologetics* by the eminent theologian Alister McGrath. So what was so significant about this moment?

For me, it highlighted that even the world's most famous atheist could not account for the nature of his moral beliefs on the basis of biology alone. By saying that his feelings about rape are simply a result of his biological and social conditioning, Dawkins affirmed that his moral beliefs are as undirected and arbitrary as any other part of the natural world. Yet you, I and Dawkins all know that rape *really is* wrong (which, I think, is why he didn't want to answer my first question), not because it happens to be where our culture has landed in its evolutionary history – after all, in some parts of the animal kingdom rape continues to be part of the natural order – but simply because *we know* that's not how humans should treat one another. But such moral knowledge only makes sense if something beyond evolution, culture and our material world can ground it. Dawkins' response confirmed again the power of the moral argument for God – the same argument that had convinced C. S. Lewis to abandon his atheism.

Evidently it was not going to convince this particular Oxford professor, but I was glad to have had a chance to at least give Dawkins a hint of the consequences of his worldview. Our ten–minute recording over, I left the gathering and practically skipped down the road, having bagged the interview I'd been waiting three years for.

THE EVOLUTION OF DAWKINS

Despite his anti-theism, I have a lot of affection for Richard Dawkins. He's been the unspoken presence on so many of the shows I've recorded, it would be hard to imagine the past ten years without him. In his early career, Dawkins was primarily known for his science. *The Selfish Gene* in 1976 and *The Extended Phenotype* in 1982 were both serious contributions to evolutionary biology. However, his works gradually became more populist and aimed at debunking religious beliefs. The publication in 2006 of his bestselling book *The God Delusion* marked a tipping point when Dawkins became better known for his anti-religious views than his science. Ever since, he has been the unofficial leader of the New Atheist movement.

My path would occasionally cross Dawkins' again in the years after our brief interview. One of the most theatrical episodes was in October 2011 when I was involved in helping to organize a debate tour for the US philosopher and notable Christian debater William Lane Craig. Premier Christian Radio was among a group of organizations hosting the tour, which included an opening night in London where I chaired a debate between Craig and the atheist philosopher Stephen Law. Over 1,700 people attended. We had hoped for the crowning moment of the tour to be a debate between Craig and Dawkins himself in the auspicious setting of the Sheldonian Theatre, Oxford. But, to our disappointment, Dawkins had turned down the invitation, just as he had on previous occasions, offering a variety of reasons for his refusal to have a debate with Craig, whom he evidently considered an unworthy opponent.

Not to be put off, the organizing committee decided to see if the arch-atheist could be persuaded. A surprising ally was found in fellow Oxford academic and atheist Daniel Came, who had written a letter to Dawkins criticizing his refusal to debate with Craig, saying: 'The absence of a debate with the foremost apologist for Christian theism is a glaring omission on your CV and is of course apt to be interpreted as cowardice on your part.' Came had pinpointed the hypocrisy of Dawkins' turning down a debate with a serious opponent yet willingly engaging with extreme and anti-intellectual Christian voices in other contexts. This suited his purposes well, as they practically made the argument against faith for themselves. A piece in *The Telegraph* newspaper, quoting from his letter, threw down the gauntlet: if Dawkins had the guts, then the invitation to meet Craig in Oxford was open.

But there was more to come. Dawkins had helped launch the atheist bus campaign in London the previous year with its slogan, 'There's probably no God. Now stop worrying and enjoy your life.' So the tour committee commissioned a tongue-in-cheek bus campaign of their own in Oxford. Had he been cycling past a bus in the weeks running up to the debate, the professor would have seen our own version of the poster, which read: 'There's probably no Dawkins. Now stop worrying and enjoy Oct 25th at the Sheldonian Theatre.'

We thought it was all in good humour. Dawkins didn't find it so funny and published an angry denunciation of William Lane Craig on the website of *The Guardian*. This was met by responses from others, such as the journalist Tim Stanley writing for *The Telegraph* in defence of Craig. It provided plenty of pre-event drama for the tour, and when the Oxford date finally came around, with the Sheldonian Theatre packed to the rafters with students, we hoped Dawkins might yet show up. An empty chair bearing his name badge was even theatrically positioned on the stage.

He didn't appear of course. So instead, Craig presented his critique of *The God Delusion*, and a panel featuring atheist and Christian academics who *were* willing to engage with the philosopher took part in a discussion with him.

To his credit, such shenanigans didn't stop Dawkins appearing on *Unbelievable?* a couple of years later (or perhaps he'd simply forgotten I was involved in the empty-chair-debate escapade). Either way, he agreed to come on by phone to be part of a friendly encounter with a Christian and Jewish contributor on the morality of the Old Testament. As expected, he made strident criticisms of the violence found in some parts and debated its historicity as well, but he also charitably affirmed the important role of the Bible in shaping Western culture, not least the impact of the King James Version on the English language. It was a healthy and helpful debate and showed that Dawkins has his mellow side too. I hope he'll come on again one day.

ATHEISM 2.0

The rise of the New Atheism has been part of a wider picture of non-belief. Notwithstanding pockets of growth in certain parts of the Church, there's no doubt that religious practice is in general decline in the West, especially among a younger generation. In the UK, church attendance has fallen from nearly 12 per cent of the population in 1980 to 5 per cent in 2015.[2] In the USA, the rise of the 'nones' – those who say they have no religious affiliation – has risen to 35 per cent of millennials (those born between 1981 and 1996).[3] But that doesn't mean the nones are necessarily adopting the strident atheism of Dawkins and co. According to Pew Research, more people than ever are reporting themselves to be 'spiritual but not religious'.[4] In fact, on a global level atheism is shrinking as a proportion of the population. In 1970, atheists made up 4.5 per cent of the world's population. That figure shrank to 2 per cent in 2010 and is projected to drop to 1.8 per cent by 2020.[5] Through both conversion and having more children, Christians, Muslims and people of other religions are proliferating at a faster rate than their non-religious counterparts in the West.

The New Atheism shone brightly in Europe and the USA for a while in the mid-2000s. Books like *God Is Not Great* by Christopher Hitchens and *The End of Faith* by Sam Harris, which poured intellectual scorn on religion, rode high in the bestseller charts. But that publishing phenomenon seems to have run its course, and nowadays the self-help spirituality of Oprah Winfrey and Deepak Chopra is back in vogue.

Ten years since the publication of *The God Delusion*, it feels as if New Atheism may have run its course too. People have tired of brash fundamentalism, whether from religious or non-religious sources. When Dawkins gets mentioned by non-believers in my studio today, it's often in the context of 'I'm not that sort of atheist, you know.' The dimming of the biologist's cultural cachet began around the same time he discovered Twitter. The social media platform has much to commend it, but has also allowed Dawkins to commit multiple gaffes. From derogatory comments about Islam to offending feminists, his postings there have caused his reputation as a public intellectual to lose its sheen. For good or ill, the history books may well remember him more for the controversial brand of atheism he championed in the twenty-first century than for the scientific achievements of his early career.

Meanwhile many atheists want to move on from bashing religion and have distanced themselves from both Dawkins and his movement. Some, like the cultural philosopher Alain de Botton, are talking about 'Atheism 2.0'. When I interviewed de Botton for *Unbelievable?* about his book *Religion for Atheists*, he didn't profess any desire to move people who were already religious out of their faith commitments. Instead he was interested in taking the trappings of religion – shared rituals, community, the reflection and pattern of life it provides – and co-opting it for non-religious people who feel cut adrift in an increasingly individualistic society.

I appreciated de Botton's aims, but couldn't agree with his methodology. A beautiful picture of the glorious and ornate arched ceiling of King's College Chapel, Cambridge, hung in the room of de Botton's flat where we conducted our conversation. It was an image that exemplified his philosophy. He explained how he could appreciate the beauty of the building without believing in the God for whose glory it was built. But taking the containers of faith – its buildings, rituals and practices – while rejecting the object at its core has always seemed an empty pursuit to me, like ripping off layers of wrapping on a present on Christmas morning only to find no gift inside, just an empty box and a mountain of waste paper around you.

I practise my faith with a diverse community of people who comprise the local church that I am part of. Churches in general are far more diverse than the sports clubs, social groups or political organizations that gather around the shared interests of similar people. People who would never normally have any reason to get together do get together at my church, and amazing things happen as a result. The diversity we see only makes sense because of the person we gather in unity around – Jesus Christ. Atheism 2.0 is still in its infancy. Whether the kind of community movement it aspires to produce will be any less like a social club or any more successful than Dawkins' brand of non-belief remains to be seen.

Nevertheless, Christians have much to thank the world's best-known atheist evangelist for. Apart from supplying plenty of material for my programme, the brand of scepticism Dawkins has spearheaded has made Christians up their game and think through their faith more critically. In the process, I'm sure he has been instrumental in some people becoming atheists. But I've equally met others who can trace his influence in their journey towards Christianity. More than anything, we can thank him for placing the God debate firmly back in the public square and revitalizing a Christian response through apologetics in the Church.

As it happens, Dawkins was also the person who invented the term 'meme'. Originally it referred to an idea that gets passed down through generations culturally in the same way that genes are passed along biologically. Nowadays the term is more likely to be associated with Internet memes – the bumper stickers of the online world. They usually comprise images with bold captions posted in Internet chat rooms or on social media timelines. In the case of the atheist meme, you can guarantee the text and image will be making a pointed objection to religion.

With that in mind it may be helpful to draw together five of the most common popular objections, not yet covered in this book, that have been popularized by the New Atheists over the past ten years or more. They may not be the best arguments, but they are the ones you will see frequently employed by atheists online. The responses here are my own and are therefore by no means the last word on the issues. Others might choose to take quite different approaches. Nevertheless, they represent the view from where I stand now.

MEME 1: ATHEISM IS SIMPLY LACK OF BELIEF IN GOD

Typically atheism has been defined as the belief that there is no God. But I've increasingly seen atheists adopt this novel definition of atheism as 'lack of belief' in God. Why is this significant?

In my opinion, it's a move aimed at pushing the burden of proof entirely on to the theist. By arguing that she merely 'lacks belief' in God, an atheist can claim that she is justified in her position until the Christian believer shows some convincing evidence that there is a God. On this rationale, atheism is the 'default' position that people are born with, until they get persuaded (or indoctrinated) to believe in God.

But I have several problems with this increasingly popular description. First, it's a definition that describes the mental state of the person, but offers no real content. Rocks, chairs and cats also lack belief in God. Does that make them atheists?

Second, it makes an atheist indistinguishable from an agnostic. Someone who hasn't yet decided whether God exists also lacks belief in God. But that's not the label atheists have adopted. So in the end, the atheist's 'lack of belief' seems to be just the same as the positive belief that there is no God. But if they do in fact hold such a belief, then it requires justification just as much as the Christian who claims there is a God.

There are variations on the theme in popular memes. One reads: 'You don't believe in Zeus, Thor or Odin. Well, I just believe in one less god than you.' This is an old chestnut that I've seen repeated by all the leading voices of New Atheism. But, rather obviously, there's a world of difference between disbelieving in a panoply of gods and moving to the belief that no supernatural cause of the universe or ultimate foundation for meaning, morality and purpose exists whatsoever. Christian philosopher Randal Rauser likens it to a bachelor telling a married man: 'You didn't marry Sheila or Tracy. Well, I just married one less woman than you.'

Another variation of the 'lack of belief' view can be illustrated in a meme attributed to atheist comedian Ricky Gervais which reads: 'Saying "Atheism is a belief system" is like saying "Not going skiing is a hobby."' My first (admittedly sarcastic) response to his analogy is that I've yet to read a bestselling book on the benefits of not going skiing. Nor have I seen many websites dedicated to disproving the existence of ski slopes. For people who merely lack belief in God, most self-declared atheists have an awful lot to say on the subject. But I also bet, if I sat down and chatted with Gervais about what his 'lack of belief' entails, there would turn out to be a great deal of content to it.

In practice, many atheists adopt naturalism, a worldview rich in metaphysical beliefs about the nature of reality. These often include: the existence of the universe and its physical laws is a brute fact that requires no explanation; there is neither purpose nor design to the universe; all that ultimately exists is physical matter and energy; life arose by chance; good and evil are human constructs . . . and so the list goes on. Yet these are all distinct claims about the nature of reality that need defending. The atheism of people like Gervais, it turns out, is a worldview just as much as Christianity. There is no 'default' position. Everyone is called to give reasons why their view of reality is the best explanation of the universe we live in.

MEME 2: GOD DIDN'T CREATE HUMANS – HUMANS CREATED GOD

This is an objection that often stems from an evolutionary explanation for why people hold supernatural beliefs. The story goes that the universal human propensity for religious beliefs has been hardwired into us because of the evolutionary benefits that God-belief offers. It acts as a communal glue, helps control social behaviour, gives explanation for things we don't understand, helps people to face the hardships of life, and so on. The atheist says we ought to transcend the superstitions of our forebears now that we know the origins of their beliefs.

In response, I'd first want to question whether this 'just so' story of the evolution of religious belief is as straightforward as portrayed. Atheists are equally likely to point out the social ills caused by religion – so which is it to be? Moreover, Christian belief is specifically tied to claims about the historical events surrounding Jesus Christ, not a fuzzy evolutionary process. More importantly, there is nothing about the positive social benefits of belief in God that is inconsistent with it being true. If God exists, then we would precisely expect belief in God to be an innate and widespread phenomenon.

Technically speaking, the objection commits the 'genetic fallacy' by assuming that showing the origin of a belief-forming process is enough to show it is false or untrustworthy. I might develop the belief that Richard Dawkins is a keen cyclist because I saw him walking into a cycle shop in Oxford, when in fact I was mistaken – it was just someone who looked like him. But my belief could still be true nevertheless (as I discovered when we had our walking conversation). The fact is that God could have intended the causal factors that brought about the processes that formed belief in our ancestors. Likewise, there are all manner of rational reasons for believing in God, such as the ones outlined in the early chapters of this book, which confirm they were correct to believe in God, even if they happened to believe for entirely different reasons.

MEME 3: SO OUT OF THE THOUSANDS OF RELIGIONS, YOURS JUST HAPPENS TO BE RIGHT?

This objection seems to imply two criticisms. First, that Christians are arrogant for believing that, among all the religious claims that exist, they possess the truth. Second is an implicit objection that, if Christianity is true, we wouldn't expect to see the diversity of other religions that exist around the world.

Of course, the first criticism cuts both ways. Atheists also believe they have the truth. The Christian might equally respond 'So out of the thousands of beliefs about the nature of the world, yours just happens to be right?' It could even be argued that Christianity is more open to diversity of beliefs than atheism. Christians can at least affirm some truths, such as the existence of a Creator God, held in common with other religions, whereas atheism denies there is truth in any religious claims. But as I mentioned in Chapter 5, I don't believe we need to treat religion like a game of roulette, nor make an exhaustive search of every religious claim. The historical evidence alone is enough to give the open-minded enquirer confidence that Jesus is who he said he was and rose from death. If we have found the key that unlocks the door to truth, our search is over.

The second objection really boils down to another version of the problem of evil. Why would a good God allow so many people to be deceived into believing in false religions? I'm not inclined to see the issue that way, however. One can just as easily see the proliferation of religion in the world as a sign that there is a shared consciousness that something beyond ourselves really exists.

The apostle Paul saw this universal awareness as a law written deep in people's hearts. When he addresses the Athenian philosophers at the Areopagus, he told them:

> I see that in every way you are very religious. For as I walked around and looked carefully at your objects of worship, I even found an altar with this inscription: TO AN UNKNOWN GOD. So you are ignorant of the very thing you worship – and this is what I am going to proclaim to you.

> (Acts 17.22–23)

In doing so, he acknowledged the universal search for God, describing the Athenians as seekers groping around for God, and even quoting their own religious poetry to them. He doesn't simply poo-poo their search. Instead he affirms it, but makes clear that the truth they have been searching for has been revealed in Jesus. In a world of free human beings influenced by our own fallen nature, we shouldn't be surprised to see many religious expressions emerge, but the Christian vision is a hopeful one – that all true searching finds its goal in Jesus Christ.

'But what about all those who perish without hearing of Jesus?' the sceptic may press. I believe that, just as John 14.6 states, Jesus is the way, the truth and the life and that nobody comes to the Father except through him. But I'm humble enough to recognize that only God is in a position to judge the heart of every true seeker, whether he or she knew the name of Christ or not. Ultimately, if God is the God of perfect justice then no one will stand before him on the final day and say 'I have been treated unfairly.' In the meantime, the present-day job of the Christian is to continue to share the life-changing news of the Christ, who is the fulfilment of all our religious searching.

MEME 4: A GOD WHO'D SEND ME TO HELL FOR NOT BELIEVING IN HIM ISN'T WORTH WORSHIPPING

The problem with this objection is that it suffers from a misconceived view of what heaven, hell and God are actually about. Too often our view of hell is more informed by medieval images of torture chambers and devils wielding red hot pokers than by Scripture itself. Equally, heaven is often envisaged as a glorified retirement home where, if we are lucky enough to get selected, we'll get to play heavenly golf for eternity. But neither of these are correct.

My best present understanding of hell from Scripture (which would take a whole book to defend properly) is one that theologians sometimes label 'annihilationism'. In a nutshell, it's a view in which hell constitutes a final end to the existence of those who refuse God's offer of salvation. It's a position that has been held by a growing number of significant Christian leaders such as John Stott, despite the prevalence of the traditional view that hell is a place of eternal conscious torment (ECT) among many of his fellow Evangelicals. Like Stott, I've personally found annihilationism both more biblically defensible and more ethically satisfying than the ECT view.

Then there's heaven. As with hell, we are always dealing with picture language, but the phrase Jesus most often used for it was 'the kingdom of heaven'. If that's so, we must ask what the defining characteristic of a kingdom is. The answer is: a king. Heaven then, according to the Bible, is a renewed creation where Jesus is king over everything. It's all about living under the perfect rule of the King. This is no glorified retirement home in the clouds, but a reality that demands heart, soul and mind, a place where those challenging Scriptures about giving up our own lives to find the true life of Christ are made utterly real.

The personal question the atheist must then ask is: 'Would I want to live there?' And that depends upon the atheist. It's not simply about believing in God. It's about whether you would want that God, even if you believed in him.

In a very honest passage, atheist philosopher Thomas Nagel writes:

> I want atheism to be true and am made uneasy by the fact
> that some of the most intelligent and well-informed people

I know are religious believers. It isn't just that I don't believe in God and, naturally, hope that I'm right in my belief. It's that I hope there is no God! I don't want there to be a God; I don't want the universe to be like that.[6]

I believe that there are plenty of people living their lives quite independently of God who, if push came to shove, would react strongly against the idea of living under the authority of anyone but themselves. I can imagine that there are people who would prefer, if they met God face to face, to continue to be their own authority. In which case, God gives them what they want – separation from him. It was C. S. Lewis who, as ever, put it most clearly and succinctly:

There are only two kinds of people in the end: those who say to God, 'Thy will be done,' and those to whom God says, in the end, 'Thy will be done.' All that are in Hell, choose it. Without that self-choice there could be no Hell. But no soul that seriously and constantly desires joy will ever miss it. Those who seek find. To those who knock it is opened.[7]

It may be that Lewis conceived of this self-chosen hell as an everlasting fate, though he also hints elsewhere at the possibility that people may change their mind and receive heaven after all. The most important point I take from his reasoning is that God won't force anyone to love him. But, as far as I can see, if people choose separation instead, and inevitably cut themselves off from the source of life itself, they have chosen a final end to their existence instead. So hell isn't God's punishment for not believing the right things; it's a self-imposed exile and final end for those who simply don't want God.

MEME 5: RELIGION IS TO BLAME FOR ALL THE EVIL AND CONFLICT IN THE WORLD

This has probably been the loudest and most persistent claim of the New Atheism. It's not just that religion is wrong, it's also dangerous. It was the view especially championed by Christopher Hitchens, the polemical journalist and speaker who was counted as one of the so-called 'four horsemen' of the New Atheism. But if Richard Dawkins, Sam Harris and Daniel Dennett were perceived to bring the cultural capital of science and philosophy, Hitchens brought the party. He was an opinionated journalist of the liberal establishment with a quick wit and a sharp tongue (often loosened by a few glasses of whisky, allegedly).

Hitchens, a heavy smoker all his life, died of oesophageal cancer in 2011. After his death, tributes poured in not only from fellow atheists but from many former foes of 'the Hitch', as he was affectionately known. However fiery he was as he delivered his views on religion, he was eminently likeable in person and counted a surprising number of conservative Christians as friends.

A year or two before the onset of his illness, I had been given the telephone number of his New York apartment. I considered inviting him to contribute to *Unbelievable?* but I never dialled the number in the end. I still regret not picking up the phone and asking him. It would have been a great show. What Hitchens wrote about the evils of religion was not so much a scholarly argument as a wave of righteous indignation. The barbs were not just reserved for Christianity. Islam, Judaism and Eastern religions were all included in the roll call of blame. His outlook was encapsulated in the title of his bestselling book, *God Is Not Great: How Religion Poisons Everything.*

But Hitchens' arguments, while drawing him a devoted following, consisted of rhetoric more than reason. As a Christian, I don't aim to defend all the forms of religion that Hitchens critiqued. I'm happy to agree with him on many instances of bad religion that he took aim at. But when it comes to Christianity, a simple survey of history will soon confirm that, far from poisoning everything, it has been responsible for masses of positive things.

The modern benefits of healthcare, education, social provision, human rights, and even literature, art and music can all be found to have roots in the Christians who were inspired to build hospitals and schools, found universities and institutions, and create great classical works of art and music. Of course, Christianity has its dark side – episodes in history when it chose to wield the sword of power rather than carry the cross of peace. But even the most cursory reading of Jesus' words in the New Testament prove that those who have killed in his name have done so against his clear command to love our enemies. Like any institution run by humans, the Church has sanctioned both good and evil. That doesn't mean Christianity is inherently evil, merely that it can be misused.

'But can you deny that religion is the main cause of war?' asks the sceptic. Yes, I can actually. This is one among many atheist myths about religions. According to research by Bradford University, only 10 per cent of all wars in the twentieth and twenty-first century have had a clear religious motivation. Even Arab–Israeli wars were judged to be primarily nationalistic, not religious. In fact, the report states that in the twentieth century, 'atheistic totalitarian states (Stalin's Russia and Mao's China) have perpetrated more mass murder than any state dominated by a religious faith'. Overall, the report noted the positive role of religion in pressing for non-violent resolution of conflicts and that 'very few if any wars in the past 100 years have been purely religious wars'.[8]

None of this is to claim that Christianity has an unblemished record. It clearly doesn't. But if we are simply tallying the comparative death counts between religious and atheistic states, the facts don't stack up on Hitchens' side at all.

There are a hundred more objections, questions and memes that we could attempt to answer, and we'd still have barely begun. That's partly why *Unbelievable?* has been going for so long. There's always a novel dispute going on somewhere on the Internet that can provide a fresh topic for conversation. But despite the endless supply of objections to religion, there's one thing which could answer them all. If God raised Jesus from death, then everything else is window dressing. If that's true, then we can work on the rest. If it's not, then I need to find myself a new job.

But I do believe there is a God, and I do believe he raised Jesus from the dead and – as I hope to show in the final chapter of this book – that changes everything.

9 Choosing to live in the Christian story of reality

The unexamined life is not worth living.

Socrates[1]

I once heard the evangelist Michael Green tell the story of a woman who found Christianity compelling in some ways, but remained uncertain about committing herself as there were various questions and issues she had yet to resolve. A friend took her to an old church and showed her the building. From the outside, it looked austere and forbidding, with tall windows that were dark and opaque. But when they approached the front door and stepped inside, the light streamed through the stained glass into the church, bathing the interior with glorious colour. The church was a very different experience from the inside.

Investigating the evidence for faith matters. It may well be an important part of someone's journey that they spend considerable time poking at Christianity from the outside. But stepping inside may make all the difference too. St Augustine is credited with the maxim *credo ut intelligam* – 'I believe in order to understand'. Likewise, some truths can only be understood when they are stepped into. I believe Christianity can only be truly appreciated once it stops being a thought system to be picked apart and becomes a way of life ready to be practised and lived.

One of the most controversial things I ever did on *Unbelievable?* was to dare atheists and agnostics to try, in a small way, stepping into the Christian worldview and see what happened. We called it the 'Atheist Prayer Experiment'. I developed the concept with Tim Mawson, a Christian philosopher at Oxford University. I had read his paper 'Praying to Stop Being an Atheist',[2] which argued that, on balance, it made sense for atheists to pray to God to reveal himself to them. It was a well-formulated and entertaining proposition, which essentially boiled down to the idea that atheists might as well try praying to God since they've got nothing to lose and potentially everything to gain. So we put the word out and invited atheists and agnostics to get in touch with us to sign up to the experiment. Over the course of 40 days (it felt like an appropriately biblical number) they would be required to pray for a couple of minutes every day for God to reveal himself to them, and record anything that happened. I was only expecting a handful of responses to this rather eccentric request, but in the end over 70 people agreed to take part.

The results were compelling listening. Of course, some people treated it as a joke, and a number dropped out of the experiment along the way. Others took it very seriously, however, and managed to complete the 40 days. Some kept a journal to record their observations; others posted their reflections on a Facebook page we created for the experiment. Some even filmed themselves praying and posted it online. So what happened?

Most of the participants said they didn't feel as if they'd had any response. For them, the experiment served to confirm their atheism. Others said that some unusual things did happen over the course of the experiment. There were those who enjoyed a sense of peace and clarity during their prayer time. A few people reported an unusual number of coincidences or significant life events happening over the time period. One person said that the experiment had left them 'open' to the idea of God. Another person who had been struggling with depression unexpectedly heard a voice in her head while she prayed, saying 'Be thankful.'[3]

The average Christian might be tempted to interpret these experiences as signs of God trying to get the attention of the atheists. Yet these phenomena were generally explained by the participant either as a natural effect of taking time to meditate or a tendency to be more alert to noticing coincidences over the course of the experiment. In the case of the 'Be thankful' voice, despite it being a welcome and helpful moment, the participant put it down to something that came from within her, rather than anywhere else.

A lot of atheists were sceptical of the whole project, but some Christians also voiced concerns. What exactly was this supposed to prove? How would we know the atheists were genuinely seeking? And why expect God to take part in such an experiment? Jesus' words in Luke chapter 4 about 'not putting God to the test' were mentioned more than once. These were all valid concerns and there was no doubt that the project pushed the envelope of what the show existed for. We had called it an experiment, though it was certainly not scientific – prayer isn't something you can analyse that way. We were simply relying on the honesty of those taking part and knew that, whether positive or negative, any results would probably tell us more about the participants than God. I also thought it couldn't do any harm to get a bunch of atheists praying for 40 days.

Interestingly, two of those who had signed up to take part did end up changing their minds about their atheism, and said they now believed in God. Kendra was already a listener to the show and said that she reached her decision to become a Christian shortly after deciding to take part in the experiment. Being given an excuse to pray seemed to suddenly open the floodgates. She wrote: 'With God I feel like I have hope and positivity. I feel safe. I feel like I have direction. I found that when I was an atheist I felt lost and alone. I just couldn't deny my belief any longer.' The other was Kelly, who was heavily pregnant when she decided to take part, and started immediately to pray every day. A few days later she went into labour, and gave birth to a healthy baby girl. Later on, she witnessed a magnificent rainbow in the sky. She took these as signs that her prayers had been answered, and believed in God from then on.

Ironically, Kendra and Kelly both came to their belief in God before the project had officially got under way. Strictly speaking, our two positive results both fell outside the official 40-day window of the trial. I personally took it as a sign of God's sense of humour about trying to be co-opted into a scientific experiment.

It was also a reminder of the fact that different people have very different expectations of what counts as evidence for God. Kendra gave into something that she couldn't deny was there any longer. For Kelly, giving birth and seeing a rainbow was enough to bring her to belief. But others reported seeing double rainbows, hearing a voice and experiencing strange coincidences, yet still didn't believe. What counts as evidence probably depends on your starting point.

Over the years most atheists I've spoken with say that they would believe in God if only there were enough evidence.

Because of that, when I've had conversations with people who seem completely unmoved by any theistic arguments, I've increasingly concluded by asking them what kind of evidence *would* cause them to believe that God exists. It often turns out, when pressed, that they find it difficult to think of anything that would actually do the job. What about seeing a limb spontaneously regenerate after prayer? Well, weird things happen biologically; I wouldn't put it down to God. How about the stars lining up to spell out 'Hello, it's me'? Well, that could be done by advanced alien technology. What if Jesus appeared in the room with you this very minute? Well, it's more likely I'd be hallucinating than something supernatural was going on. And so on. There are some people whose 'skept-o-meter'[4] is dialled so high that everything, however improbable, must have a naturalistic explanation by default.

It also feeds into a question that sometimes gets asked by both atheists and Christians. Why doesn't God simply make his existence obvious to everyone? If he is there, why does he hide himself? Having devoted my life to hosting hundreds of debates on the evidence, I've come to a rather shocking conclusion.

Maybe God isn't interested in people simply believing in him.

Instead, I think God is far more interested in people loving him and trusting him than merely believing in him. Forcing himself on people with an undeniable demonstration of his existence would, at some level, rob humans of their ability to choose him, trust him and love him. One of the most important lessons in my own Christian walk has been learning to 'live by faith, not by sight' (2 Corinthians 5.7). That may sound like a cliché to the sceptic. But I honestly believe that part of what makes us fully human is our capacity to develop patience, love, moral virtue, fortitude and wisdom through learning to trust in a God we cannot see. I think it's what Jesus had in mind when he said to Thomas (another famous sceptic): 'blessed are those who have not seen and yet have believed' (John 20.29). In the end, faith is not merely about belief; it's about learning to trust the God we cannot see to make sense of the world we can.

APOLOGETICS IS NOT THE POINT

You have reached the final chapter in an apologetics book. My aim has been to show you that, despite various competing options and worldviews, especially that of atheism, Christianity makes best sense of the world we inhabit. That's what apologetics is about, but it's really only the beginning of the story. I believe that the truth of the Christian faith is most fully confirmed when you put it into practice, step inside the church and see it from the inside. Having spelled out my case for Christianity, I want to use this final chapter to talk about what it means to actually step inside the reality of that faith.

You've probably worked out that I'm a big fan of apologetics. When done well, it's an excellent way to engage those who are unconvinced or antagonistic towards the gospel. At the same time, I've also seen certain dangers in apologetics. If not grounded in prayer and humility, it can easily breed a form of arrogance and intellectual idolatry. If apologetics leads only to a change in our heads and not our hearts, then we have missed the real goal.

Like the *Star Wars* collector who keeps his original 1979 Millennium Falcon toy pristine and unopened in its original box, and has never actually played with it, too many apologists are guilty of spending more time arguing for the truth of their faith than experiencing its living reality. I sometimes fear that those non-believers whose only exposure to Christianity is a weekly dose of the *Unbelievable?* podcast may assume that debating the theories, doctrines and truth claims of Christianity is the main point. But it really isn't. I would rather have Christians with imperfect theology who go and love people in the name of Christ, than believers with perfect theology whose faith is hermetically sealed from actually making a difference. In 1 Corinthians chapter 13, St Paul likens such loveless belief to the hollow clanging of a cymbal.

What begins in the head should eventually become a matter of the heart. Sadly, apologetics can often end up resembling a game of chess in which clever moves advance an argument, but the victory amounts to little more than an intellectual exercise. Yet people can't entrust their lives to an argument, however well made. Faith involves more than that. If our arguments are worth making, it is because they open the door to trusting in a person – Jesus Christ – and then living our lives in the light of that reality.

Too often the head and the heart are played off against one another. The experientialist may say: 'I can't build my life upon the cold logic of philosophy and the shifting sands of evidential arguments. I simply trust in what God has revealed to my heart.' The evidentialist may be tempted to respond: 'I'm sick of Christians who believe in God on the basis of emotions. I need arguments and evidence to believe things in the real world, and the same applies to my faith.'

Of course, both are right. There is a tendency for people who embrace the field of apologetics to side with the evidentialist in this imagined argument, concerned as they are to rebut the arguments of their sceptical opponents. But apologetics alone can never provide the whole picture in our search for faith. In the end, nobody gets argued into the kingdom of God.

I prefer to see apologetics as a way of removing barriers to belief. If we imagine a road which a person needs to walk down in order to arrive at the goal of trusting in Jesus Christ, there may be numerous roadblocks in the way. It may be that the problem of evil and suffering in the world poses a significant hindrance. Perhaps the historical reliability of the accounts of Christ are in doubt, or the obstacle may concern whether religion does more harm than good in the world. The type of roadblocks will vary from person to person. However, with persuasive arguments we may be able to remove these obstacles one by one. If we can show that none of those objections need constitute an insurmountable obstacle, then the road may be clear enough for the person to walk towards faith in Christ. But here's the catch. They still have to be willing to walk down that road. No argument will force them to do that.

Or to use another metaphor: you can lead a horse to water but you can't make it drink. Our arguments may lead someone to the water's edge, but they have to be thirsty in order to want to drink what's on offer. In my experience, those who have come to faith via apologetics have often been drawn to the water all along; they just needed the time to sort through some of the issues. Those who don't want the water in the first place will never be compelled by arguments alone – there will always be another counterargument or objection to reach for. But for those who do want the living water where the head and the heart meet, a powerful new experience can emerge as they open themselves to the possibility of a God who was on the road with them all along.

CHRISTIANITY WORKS

I've been privileged to be able to make a living doing something that I love – radio broadcasting. What I've learned from sitting in front of a microphone to record hundreds of conversations on faith for *Unbelievable?* has ultimately convinced me that the balance of evidence is on the side of God and Christianity. But seeing the practical reality of Christian faith began further back, in the more humble setting of thatched mud-and-straw huts in Africa, with scrawny chickens scratching outside in the dust.

Before settling down into the adult world of jobs, house and family commitments, Lucy and I decided to begin our married life with a gap year spent working for an Anglican mission agency in Namibia, on the south-west coast of Africa. Despite its large size, the country is relatively sparsely populated, consisting most-ly of beautiful but arid desert land. There are more seals on the coastal shorelines than people in the country itself. We were based in the north of the country where the population is concen-trated, living on a remote mission station that serves the rural area around it.

In the course of our stay at the Odibo mission, we made friends with many of the local Ovambo people. We taught their children in school and sat with them in their homesteads to eat *oshifima* porridge and to drink (or try to drink) murky home-brewed *oshikundu* beer, both made from the staple millet crop known locally as *omahangu*. And yes, nearly everything begins with the letter 'o'. We also prayed and sang beside them every Sunday in church services that would frequently last five hours or more. Most people lived a subsistence lifestyle, dependent on a few weeks of annual rain that would turn the desert green for a month and ensure the harvest for the coming year. In material terms, they lived in relative poverty compared to the Western lifestyle we knew, but we have never met more generous people in our lives.

Christianity reached the northern tribes of Namibia in the late nineteenth century. The legacy of colonialism in the country was complicated, with both positive and negative effects in a country that was one of the last African nations to declare independence, in 1990. Nevertheless, I found it impossible to deny the positive effects that had come with Christian faith – education, poverty relief, healthcare, rights for women and children. The long-established mission station with its hospital, school and church serving the local areas was a living example of the impact. More than that, I also witnessed how the spiritual core of Christianity had been embraced culturally and personally in the lives of those we met. As a husband and wife descended from Anglo-Saxon tribes, we embraced men and women from the Ovambo tribe as brothers and sisters. Namibian or English, we all belonged to a wider tribe – the Christian Church – which transcended our cultural and racial differences.

For me, part of the wonder of the gospel is that it can be simple enough for a child to grasp yet deep enough for the wisest sage to spend his or her life contemplating. It also has an uncanny ability to speak to every place, people and time. It can transform nations without crushing their culture. In Namibia, many of the expressions of faith by Christians there were different from our own (not least the length of the church services), but even these were a sign of Christianity's inherent flexibility for cultural accommodation that has allowed it not just to exist, but thrive, across the entire world. Despite the frequent headlines about the decline of Christendom in the West, Christianity is growing faster than ever before in Africa, Asia, Latin America and parts of the Middle East.

Os Guinness, countering the postmodern idea that things can 'be true for you but not for me' has written: 'the Christian faith is not true because it works; it works because it is true.'[5]

That idea was confirmed for me in Namibia. Wherever it takes root, Christianity has an ennobling effect on those who embrace its authentic core. Those who are driven by its story of a God of gracious and unconditional love, made known in Jesus Christ, have reshaped entire nations in ways that politics, power and economic programmes have been unable to. Many ethical systems and ideologies profess grand ideals, and a desire to change the world for the better. Only Christianity actually delivers on its promises, because it begins by transforming individuals.

Years later, I read an article in *The Times* by Matthew Parris, surprisingly titled 'As an Atheist, I Truly Believe Africa Needs God'.[6] Following a trip to Malawi where he had lived as a child, he was confronted by the impact Christianity had made in the intervening 45 years. He explained why, despite it sitting awkwardly with his atheism, he couldn't deny the inward spiritual and outward social change he witnessed among individuals and communities in Africa in ways that NGOs and foreign aid could not hope to match. Parris doesn't believe in Christianity, but he believes it works. I'd go one step further. The fact that Christianity works is a clue to the fact that it really is true. This is still apologetics of course – showing that there is a practical fit between Christianity and the world. But to see truly that Christianity works requires us to step daringly into a new story of reality that will change both us and the world, as we move from mere belief to living faith.

STEPPING INTO THE STORY OF GOD

C. S. Lewis famously wrote: 'I believe in Christianity as I believe that the sun has risen: not only because I see it, but because by it I see everything else.'[7]

What we believe about the world and how we interact with it will very much depend on the worldview that we adopt. When I put my contact lenses in my eyes every morning, suddenly the blurry outlines of my house become clear and distinct. If I then put on a pair of sunglasses as I step outside into bright sunlight, my view of the world will change again. Inhabiting a Christian, atheist or other religious worldview is somewhat like putting on a pair of glasses that changes our focus. The worldview different people adopt might just as easily be an unexamined Western consumerism or strongly held political ideology. Whatever our worldview may be, none of us have unimpeded 20/20 vision when it comes to the true picture of reality. Our assumptions, beliefs and values act as a filter through which we interpret and engage the world around us.

In the Christian worldview, intellectual arguments and evidence may help us to establish the fact that God exists and has been revealed in Jesus Christ. But the real task of faith is coming to see the whole world through Christ-focused spectacles. That's why my experience of seeing Christianity working in Africa is as important as the evidence delivered to me by history, science and philosophy. My Christian faith causes me to look at the world differently because it lights the world up in a new way. Many of my atheist friends live in a story in which there is no overarching narrative, no ultimate purpose. To them, our brief human life is a lucky accident in an otherwise meaningless cosmos, and so we make the most of it while we can. In contrast, as a Christian I have chosen to live within a very different story about reality. It's one in which there is a God who purposes every life, invests it with ultimate value, and calls us to be part of a grand narrative that is being woven through time, space and the whole of human history.

It is a story that is reflected across the sweep of Scripture in four main acts – Creation, Fall, Redemption and Restoration. A very quick overview of the four acts might run like this: Creation – the world was created good, and humans bear God's image and are made to be in relationship with him; Fall – but things went wrong because people preferred to live by their own rules, leading to death, decay, and discord with God and one another; Redemption – God still loves us, but because our own efforts to reach up to him are futile he comes down in person to suffer the consequences of our rebellion so that we can be restored to relationship with him; Restoration – Christ's resurrection is the foretaste of the world to come when death will be turned back and all things put right. Here and now, those who trust in Christ are tasked with joining him in bringing the kingdom-yet-to-come into the present reality as we walk in faith and obedience with him.

One of the most surprising validations of the beauty of that story came early in the life of *Unbelievable?* when I interviewed for the first time a significantly anti-religious atheist named John Loftus. He had once been a committed believer who was involved in Christian leadership but, after falling out with his church following an affair and then coming to doubt the claims of Christianity, he lost his faith. He would prove to be even more evangelistic as an atheist, writing books and maintaining a website dedicated to debunking Christianity.

Yet after spelling out his reasons for rejecting Christianity across an entire show, Loftus ended by telling me, almost wistfully, that the hardest part of becoming an atheist was losing the Christian story:

> The story itself was amazing. There is no other story like it of a God who comes down as his Son, dies on the cross for our sins, resurrects from the grave and gives us hope. There is no other story in the world that is more beautiful than that one.[8]

I was struck by the fact that even an atheist as strong in his convictions as Loftus could still recognize the beauty of the Christian story that had once captivated him.

I don't think that you need to be a believer to see that the world resonates with the grand narrative of Creation, Fall, Redemption and Restoration. The beauty and order of the created world continues to inspire a transcendent sense of wonder in people with or without faith. Whether you believe in the idea of 'the Fall' or not, one only needs to turn on the TV or read a newspaper to see that the world is not as it should be and that evil really exists. Likewise, most people believe that there's a direction that humanity should be travelling in. Every song about love lost and won, and every film about good overcoming evil is an echo of that greater story of redemption. And then there's death, the one inevitable reality we are all guaranteed, and yet the one thing we spend most of our resources, money and time striving to delay, escape or forget. We long for resurrection and restoration, and sit strangely at odds with the dying world we currently find ourselves in. St Paul called death 'the last enemy' and, believer or not, we somehow all know what he means.

Our search then is not merely to ascertain the correct facts about God's existence and whether Jesus rose from the dead. We are all searching for the answer that unlocks the riddle of life and how it is to be lived. If God exists and Jesus rose, then the key is within our grasp, and it changes everything. God invites us to be part of his grand story of restoration by inviting us into a new reality of resurrection in Christ that will culminate in a recreated world where the King reigns once more. But until that day, journeying in Christian faith is about coming to see the whole of this life through the story of his life.

It's a version of reality where we don't have to resign ourselves to a universe of blind, pitiless indifference. Instead it's a story in which every life matters to God, where no situation is hopeless and no person too ruined by his or her past to be restored. I've seen that come true in the lives of many people who have told me about their journey. From former gangsters, prostitutes, addicts, runaways and gamblers to the everyday accounts of lives that were once drifting without an anchor, there are literally millions of stories of restoration which reflect the big story.

It is a story in which forgiveness happens against all the odds so that, at the post-apartheid Truth and Reconciliation hearings in South Africa, a black woman could embrace the white police officer who killed her son and husband, because she believes in grace. It is a story where people, inspired by the promise of a new world, have set about remaking it now. From groups of Christians in the UK who patrol the streets looking after booze-fuelled

Saturday-night clubbers, to church-led micro-finance projects in South America aimed at lifting communities out of poverty, the world is full of people living out the Christian story of redemption and restoration, because that's the way they see the world.

It's a story which produces hope-filled people who don't shrink from facing evil because they have the hope of resurrection with Christ, even if they die. Modern-day martyrs like Maximilian Kolbe and Dietrich Bonhoeffer, who gave up their own lives in the Second World War in order to save others, did so because of the story they inhabited. Their stories powerfully mirrored Christ's own story.

It is a story that speaks to our emotions and makes sense of our soul. It will tell us who we are, why we're here, how we've failed and what love has done to bring us back again. It frees us from fear, releases us from shame, and grounds our identity in a hope that never fades. It is the story to which all other stories point.

Every day, in a thousand ways, people choose to live within a certain story of reality, be it atheism, Christianity or something else. Some do it without ever asking whether their story is true, even though they base their entire lives upon it. I have aimed to show that the Christian story is the true one. And I hope that, in some small way, I may have persuaded you that living in that story is what really matters.

ONCE AGAIN, CONVERSATIONS MATTER

Writing a book that defends the claims of Christianity, against the objections of sceptics, involves the constant danger of coming across as dismissive or arrogant towards the other side. There is always a temptation to paint opponents in harsher brushstrokes than they deserve and erect easy-to-knock-down 'straw men' in place of their actual arguments. In detailing some of the conversations I have had with sceptics, I hope I have represented the encounters fairly and, above all, not given the impression that I disliked any of them. I've certainly disagreed with them, often. But I have always enjoyed interacting with the atheists I have met, both on the show and beyond it.

Like any assortment of human beings gathered under a banner, atheists, agnostics and sceptics are a diverse bunch. Some have been inflammatory, while others have been a model of graciousness. Some expressed emotional outrage in their case against God, while others employed dispassionate logic. Some have major problems with religion, while others have praised the benefits of believing. Some find Christians arrogant and annoying, while others find other atheists arrogant and annoying. Some came to have a fight; others came to listen and learn. Some seem to hate the very notion of God; others desperately want to believe but find themselves unable to. And they've all been worth talking to.

I've learned a great deal from the Christian guests who have sat on one side of the discussion table over the years, but I've learned just as much from the non-Christians. I have been regularly challenged, surprised and made uncomfortable in the process of talking with them. But I can also thank them, because the conversations have always caused me to take a longer, harder look at my faith, and ask 'Does this make sense?' In the end, I have found it does.

Throughout the journey, my quarrel has not been with the atheists, but with atheism. Having examined it from various angles, I have been unable to reconcile it with the world I find myself in. It's a world that is both mechanical and magical, beautiful yet broken, driven by natural laws yet teeming, just below the surface, with the presence of something altogether supernatural. In the end, Christianity still makes the most sense of life, the universe and everything.

Whether you have come to this book as a Christian or not, I hope that it has helped to give a window into my own faith and the reasons many others have also given for believing that Christianity is true. If you are a Christian, I hope that it will give you confidence in the claims of the faith you hold. And if you are not a Christian, my prayer is that it may provide you with just enough reason to move from examining the outside of the building, to walking up to the front door and taking a step inside.

Notes

INTRODUCTION

1 <https://twitter.com/peterboghossian/status/477980921711583232>.

1 CREATING BETTER CONVERSATIONS

1 <www.youtube.com/watch?v=agRu8SZRMME>.
2 <www.youtube.com/watch?v=XF9uo_P0nNI>.
3 'The Mark Driscoll Interview', special podcast, *Unbelievable?*, 14 January 2012.
4 <www.timothykeller.com/blog/2012/7/10/how-the-gospel-changes-our-apologetics-part-1>.
5 C. S. Lewis, 'Is Theism Important?', in *God in the Dock: Essays on Theology and Ethics* (Grand Rapids, MI: Eerdmans, 2014), p. 187.

2 GOD MAKES SENSE OF HUMAN EXISTENCE

1 'Science, the Universe and the God Question – John Lennox and Lawrence Krauss', *Unbelievable?*, 21 September 2013.
2 *A Debate on the Existence of God – Bertrand Russell and Father Frederick Copleston*, BBC Radio, 28 January 1948.
3 As reported by physicist Sean Carroll in 2014: <www.preposterous universe.com/blog/2014/02/24/post-debate-reflections>.

4 Alex Vilenkin, *Many Worlds in One: The Search for Other Universes* (New York: Hill & Wang, 2006), p. 176.

5 'Is the Fine-Tuning of the Universe Evidence for God? – Robin Collins vs Peter Millican', *Unbelievable?*, 18 March 2016.

6 Paul Davies, 'How Bio-Friendly Is the Universe?', 2003: <https://arxiv.org/pdf/astro-ph/0403050.pdf>.

7 Fred Hoyle, 'The Universe: Past and Present Reflections', *Engineering and Science*, November 1981, pp. 8–12 (here p. 12).

8 <http://stephenlaw.blogspot.co.uk/2007/07/improbable-universe.html>.

9 'How a Dice Can Show that God Exists': <www.youtube.com/watch?v=yy6kaDaeDT8>.

10 'Who's Afraid of the Multiverse? – Jeff Zweerink and Skydive Phil', *Unbelievable?*, 17 September 2016.

11 Eugene Wigner, 'The Unreasonable Effectiveness of Mathematics in the Natural Sciences', Richard Courant lecture in mathematical sciences delivered at New York University, 11 May 1959.

12 'Who Invented the Universe? – Alister McGrath and Jim Al-Khalili', *Unbelievable?*, 10 October 2015.

3 GOD MAKES SENSE OF HUMAN VALUE

1 With thanks to Mark Rocques who introduced me to the story of Jaime Jaramillo.

2 <www.un.org/en/universal-declaration-human-rights>.

3 'The Atheist Bus Campaign', *Unbelievable?*, 1 November 2008.

4 C. S. Lewis, *Mere Christianity* (London: HarperCollins, 2002), p. 38.

5 Leah Libresco, CNN interview, June 2012.

6 Ravi Zacharias: <www.reasonablefaith.org/media/top-five-questions-university-of-iowa-students-ask-about-christianity>.

7 <www.reasonablefaith.org/media/what-is-the-euthyphro-dilemma-bobby-conway>.

8 Endorsements at the British Humanist Association website: <www.humanism.org>.

9 'Does Humanism Need God? – Angus Ritchie vs Stephen Law', *Unbelievable?*, 17 January 2015.

10 <http://iheu.org/humanism/the-amsterdam-declaration>.

11 Angus Ritchie, 'The Apologist: Why Humanists Should Be Christians', *Premier Christianity* magazine, June 2015.

4 GOD MAKES SENSE OF HUMAN PURPOSE

1 <www.youtube.com/watch?v=rA3n2zZlLdw>.

2 The Script, 'Science and Faith', from the album *Science and Faith* (RCA, 2010).

3 Coldplay, 'A Sky Full of Stars', from the album *Ghost Stories* (Parlophone, 2014).

4 <www.google.com/trends/2014/story/top-questions.html>.

5 Richard Dawkins, *River out of Eden: A Darwinian View of Life* (London: Weidenfeld & Nicolson, 1995), p. 133.

6 C. S. Lewis, 'Is Theology Poetry?', 1944: <www.samizdat.qc.ca/arts/lit/Theology=Poetry_CSL.pdf>, pp. 14–15.

7 C. S. Lewis, *Mere Christianity* (London: HarperCollins, 2002), p. 136.

8 Andy Bannister, *The Atheist Who Didn't Exist: Or: The Dreadful Consequences of Bad Arguments* (Oxford: Monarch, 2015), p. 185.

9 Francis Spufford, *Unapologetic: Why, Despite Everything, Christianity Can Still Make Surprising Emotional Sense* (London: Faber & Faber, 2012), pp. 8–9.

10 'Does Christianity Make Emotional Sense? – Francis Spufford and Philip Pullman', *Unbelievable?*, 12 December 2012.

11 C. S. Lewis, *Mere Christianity* (London: HarperCollins, 2002), p. 134.

12 Bertrand Russell, 'A Free Man's Worship', 1903: <http://bertrandrussell.org/html/brs_russell_texts/br-fmw.html>.

13 'Can Atheists Have Meaning without God? – Michael Ruse and Andy Bannister', *Unbelievable?*, 29 August 2015.

14 'How Can I Be Happy? Narrated by Stephen Fry – That's Humanism!': <www.youtube.com/watch?v=Tvz0mmF6NW4>.

15 Holly Ordway, 'Why I Am a Christian', *Premier Christianity* magazine, August 2013.

16 C. S. Lewis, 'Meditation in a Toolshed', in *God in the Dock: Essays on Theology and Ethics* (Grand Rapids, MI: Eerdmans, 2014), pp. 230–4 (here p. 231).

5 WILL THE REAL JESUS PLEASE STAND UP?

1 Justin Brierley, 'Will the Real Jesus Please Stand Up?', *Premier Christianity* magazine, January 2014.

2 Reza Aslan, *Zealot: The Life and Times of Jesus of Nazareth* (London: The Westbourne Press), epigraph.

3 <http://historicaljesusresearch.blogspot.co.uk/2013/07/a-usually-happy-fellow-reviews-aslans.html>.

4 'Was Jesus Just a . . . Zealot? – Reza Aslan vs Anthony Le Donne', *Unbelievable?*, 14 December 2013.

5 Ariel Sabar, 'The Unbelievable Tale of Jesus' Wife', *The Atlantic*, July 2016.

6 Brierley, 'Will the Real Jesus Please Stand Up?'.

7 Barna's 'Talking Jesus' survey: <www.talkingjesus.org>.

8 'Did Jesus Exist? – Bart Ehrman Q&A', *Unbelievable?*, 18 August 2012.

9 'Did Jesus Exist? – Richard Carrier vs Mark Goodacre', *Unbelievable?*, 15 December 2012.

10 'Is There Evidence for Jesus' Life and Death?': <http://player.premier.org.uk/media/t/1_luyc1i4c/13106411>.

11 'Richard Bauckham on the Gospels, Part 1', *Unbelievable?*, 29 August 2009.

12 'Is There Evidence for Jesus' Life and Death?'.

13 C. S. Lewis, *Mere Christianity* (London: HarperCollins, 2002), p. 52.

6 FACTS THAT ONLY FIT THE RESURRECTION

1 <www.independent.co.uk/news/people/profiles/richard-dawkins-you-ask-the-questions-special-427003.html>.

2 Seventy-five per cent of scholars support arguments for the empty tomb. Gary Habermas, 'Resurrection Research from 1975 to the Present: What Are Critical Scholars Saying?', *Journal for the Study of the Historical Jesus* 3:2, 2005, pp. 135–53.

3 Gerd Lüdemann, *What Really Happened to Jesus: A Historical Approach to the Resurrection* (Louisville, KY: Westminster John Knox Press, 1995), p. 80.

4 Gary R. Habermas and Michael R. Licona, *The Case for the Resurrection of Jesus* (Grand Rapids, MI: Kregel, 2004), p. 65.

5 André Aleman and Frank Laroi, *Hallucinations: The Science of Idiosyncratic Perception* (Washington, DC: APA, 2008).

6 'Bart Ehrman on His Loss of Faith', *Unbelievable?*, 27 August 2011.

7 'New Testament Q&A – Gary Habermas and James Crossley', *Unbelievable?*, 7 August 2015.

8 'Do the Minimal Facts Support the Resurrection? – Gary Habermas and James Crossley', *Unbelievable?*, 31 July 2015.

9 'Biblical Evidence for the Resurrection – Bart Ehrman and Mike Licona', *Unbelievable?*, 16 April 2011.

7 THE ATHEIST'S GREATEST OBJECTION: SUFFERING

1 'The Young Atheist's Handbook – Alom Shaha and Tom Price', *Unbelievable?*, 24 August 2012.

2 C. S. Lewis, *Mere Christianity* (London: HarperCollins, 2002), pp. 38–9.

3 <www.premierchristianity.com/Past-Issues/2016/December-2016/My-4-year-old-son-got-brain-cancer.-But-God-isn-t-to-blame>.

4 'Why Suffering? – Sharon Dirckx and Alom Shaha', *Unbelievable?*, 16 March 2013.

5 C. S. Lewis, *The Problem of Pain* (San Francisco: HarperSanFrancisco, 2001), p. 91.

6 <www.premierchristianity.com/Past-Issues/2015/September-2015/The-rainbow-through-the-rain>.

7 <www.premierchristianradio.com/Shows/Saturday/Unbelievable/Videos/Dear-Stephen-I-Believe-In-Oscar-Wilde-s-God>.

8 Oscar Wilde, *The Selfish Giant* (London: Bloomsbury, 2000).

8 MY TEN MINUTES WITH RICHARD DAWKINS

1 'Richard Dawkins and John Lennox Debate', *Unbelievable?*, 8 November 2008.

2 <https://faithsurvey.co.uk/uk-christianity.html>.

3 <www.pewresearch.org/fact-tank/2015/05/12/millennials-increasingly-are-driving-growth-of-nones>.

4 <www.pewresearch.org/fact-tank/2016/01/21/americans-spirituality>.

5 <wwwgordonconwell.com/netcommunity/CSGCResources/ChristianityinitsGlobalContext.pdf>.

6 Thomas Nagel, *The Last Word* (New York: Oxford University Press, 1997), p. 130.

7 C. S. Lewis, *The Great Divorce* (London: HarperCollins, 1946), pp. 66–7.

8 Greg Austin, Todd Kranock and Thom Oommen, *God and War: An Audit and an Explanation* (Bradford: Bradford University Press, 2003), pp. 17, 40.

9 CHOOSING TO LIVE IN THE CHRISTIAN STORY OF REALITY

1 From Plato's *Apology*, a saying attributed to Socrates while on trial.

2 T. J. Mawson, 'Praying to Stop Being an Atheist', *International Journal for Philosophy of Religion* 67:3, 2010, pp. 173–86.

3 For the results, interviews with participants and programmes reflecting on the Atheist Prayer Experiment, visit <www.premier.org.uk/atheistprayerexperiment>.

4 With thanks to apologist David Wood for this term.

5 Os Guinness, *Time for Truth: Living Free in a World of Lies, Hype, and Spin* (Grand Rapids, MI: Baker, 2000), pp. 79–80.

6 Matthew Parris, *The Times*, 27 December 2008.

7 C. S. Lewis, 'Is Theology Poetry?', an essay presented to the Oxford Socratic Club, Oxford University, November 1944.

8 'Why I Became an Atheist, Part 1 – John Loftus and Peter May', *Unbelievable?*, 5 April 2008.

References

Aslan, Reza, *Zealot: The Life and Times of Jesus of Nazareth* (London: The Westbourne Press, 2013).

Atwill, Joseph, *Caesar's Messiah: The Roman Conspiracy to Invent Jesus* (Charleston, SC: CreateSpace, 2011).

Bannister, Andrew, *The Atheist Who Didn't Exist: Or: The Dreadful Consequences of Bad Arguments* (Oxford: Monarch, 2015).

Bauckham, Richard, *Jesus and the Eyewitnesses: The Gospels as Eyewitness Testimony* (Grand Rapids, MI: Eerdmans, 2006).

Bell, Rob, *Love Wins: A Book about Heaven, Hell, and the Fate of Every Person Who Ever Lived* (New York: HarperOne, 2011).

Botton, Alain de, *Religion for Atheists: A Non-Believer's Guide to the Uses of Religion* (London: Penguin, 2012).

Brown, Dan, *The Da Vinci Code* (New York: Anchor, 2nd edn, 2009).

Chopra, Deepak, *Jesus: A Story of Enlightenment* (New York: HarperOne, 2008).

Dawkins, Richard, *The Extended Phenotype* (Oxford: Oxford University Press, 1982).

Dawkins, Richard, *The God Delusion* (London: Bantam, 2006).

Dawkins, Richard, *The Selfish Gene* (New York: Oxford University Press, 1976).

Ehrman, Bart D., *Did Jesus Exist? The Historical Argument for Jesus of Nazareth* (New York: HarperOne, 2012).

Ehrman, Bart D., *Misquoting Jesus: The Story behind Who Changed the Bible and Why* (New York: HarperOne, 2007).

Fulwiler, Jennifer, *Something Other Than God: How I Passionately Sought Happiness and Accidentally Found It* (San Francisco: Ignatius Press, 2014).

Habermas, Gary R. and Michael R. Licona, *The Case for the Resurrection of Jesus* (Grand Rapids, MI: Kregel, 2004).

Harris, Sam, *The End of Faith: Religion, Terror, and the Future of Reason* (London: Simon & Schuster, 2006).

Hitchens, Christopher, *God Is Not Great: How Religion Poisons Everything* (London: Atlantic, 2008).

Kelley, Jessica, *Lord Willing? Wrestling with God's Role in My Child's Death* (Harrisonburg, VA: Herald Press, 2016).

Krauss, Lawrence, *A Universe from Nothing: Why There Is Something Rather Than Nothing* (London: Simon & Schuster, 2012).

Le Donne, Anthony, *The Wife of Jesus: Ancient Texts and Modern Scandals* (London: Oneworld, 2013).

Lewis, C. S., *The Great Divorce* (London: William Collins, 2015).

Lewis, C. S., *Mere Christianity* (London: William Collins, 2016).

Lewis, C. S., *Miracles* (London: William Collins, 2016).

Lewis, C. S., *The Problem of Pain* (London: William Collins, 2015).

Lewis, C. S., *Surprised by Joy* (London: William Collins, 2016).

Lewis, C. S., *The Weight of Glory: A Collection of Lewis' Most Moving Addresses* (London: William Collins, 2013).

Licona, Michael R., *Why Are There Differences in the Gospels? What We Can Learn from Ancient Biography* (New York: Oxford University Press, 2007).

McGrath, Alister, *Mere Apologetics* (London: SPCK, 2016).

Morison, Frank, *Who Moved the Stone?* (Milton Keynes: Authentic Media, 2006).

Ordway, Holly, *Not God's Type: An Atheist Academic Lays Down Her Arms* (San Francisco: Ignatius Press, 2014).

Pullman, Philip, His Dark Materials: *The Golden Compass; The Subtle Knife; The Amber Spyglass* (New York: Knopf, 1996; 1997; 2000).

Shaha, Alom, *The Young Atheist's Handbook: Lessons for Living a Good Life without God* (London: Biteback, 2012).

Spufford, Francis, *Unapologetic: Why, Despite Everything, Christianity Can Still Make Surprising Emotional Sense* (London: Faber & Faber, 2012).

Strobel, Lee, *The Case for Christ: A Journalist's Personal Investigation of the Evidence for Jesus* (Grand Rapids, MI: Zondervan, 2013).

Wilde, Oscar, *The Selfish Giant* (London: Bloomsbury, 2000).

Premier at a glance

Premier Christian Communications started as a London-based radio station. More than 20 years later, it is a flourishing multi-media organization across radio, magazines and interactive websites with on-demand video and audio.

Premier exists to enable people to put their faith at the heart of daily life and bring Christ to their communities. We support people on their faith journeys and help them to put their faith into action by providing spiritual nourishment and resources.

With an audience of more than one million people every week across the different media platforms, Premier represents a strong Christian voice in the UK. Part of what we do is to campaign on issues of concern to all Christians. Recent campaigns have included e-safety (SafetyNet), slavery (Not For Sale) and the ongoing issues with ISIS (Stop the Genocide), bringing the Christian voice to those in power.

ON RADIO

Premier Christian Radio nationally on DAB digital radio, Freeview Channel 725, in Greater London and Surrey on 1305, 1332, 1413, 1566 MW.

Premier Gospel on DAB in Greater London.

Premier Praise on national DAB digital radio.

There is an app for smartphones, and all stations can be listened to online.

IN PRINT

Premier Christianity magazine helps you to connect with God, culture and other Christians through articles, features and interviews.

Premier Youth and Children's Work magazine provides ideas, resources and guidance for those who work in children's and youth ministry.

ONLINE

The website www.premier.org.uk is a gateway to content from all Premier brands, reflecting what is on air and in print, and reacting quickly to current events. It includes video content of music, debates and interviews, Bible readings and thoughts.

Premier also offers:

Premier Lifeline – a confidential telephone listening service for support and prayer on 0300 111 0101;

Premier Life – an online lifestyle magazine inspiring people to make the most of life and its ups and downs;

Premier Jobsearch – for those looking for roles in the Christian, charitable or caring sectors;

Premier Digital – providing resources to inspire, equip and connect Christians with digital technology.

UNBELIEVABLE?

Premier's flagship apologetics debate show airs on Saturdays at 2.30 p.m. and is a popular podcast. Justin Brierley also hosts Unbelievable? The Conference annually. For the latest shows and resources, visit www.premierchristianradio.com/Shows/Saturday/Unbelievable.